inQuire within

24 visualizations for creativity & growth

VOLUME ONE

inQuire within

within

24 visualizations for creativity & growth

VOLUME ONE

Andrew E. Schwartz

Photographs by Darcy Dziedzic

Whole Person Associates Inc
Duluth, Minnesota

Whole Person Associates Inc
210 West Michigan
Duluth MN 55802-1908
218-727-0500

Inquire Within
24 Visualizations for Creativity & Growth, Volume One

Printed in the United States of America by Versa Press
10 9 8 7 6 5 4 3 2 1

Publisher: Donald A Tubesing
Editorial Director: Susan Gustafson
Manuscript Editor: Patrick Gross
Designer: Joy Morgan Dey

Library of Congress Cataloging-in-Publication Data

Schwartz, Andrew E.
    Inquire within : 24 visualizations for creativity & growth /
Andrew E. Schwartz ; photographs by Darcy Dziedzic.
        p.   cm.
    Includes bibliographical references.
    ISBN 0-938586-74-2 (v. 1 : pbk.) : $19.95
    1. Imagery (Psychology)   2. Imagery (Psychology)—
Problems, exercises, etc. 3. Visualization. 4. Meditation.
5. Self-actualization (Psychology)   I. Title.
BF367.S38   1993
153.3'2—dc20   93-6509

Dedication

To those I have loved
and
those who have taught me about love

Leonard Schwartz, Henriette Schwartz,
and Amy Rotberg Schwartz

Thank you!

About the author

Andrew E. Schwartz is president of A. E. Schwartz & Associates, a management and employee development training and consulting organization, based in Watertown, Massachusetts, that offers over forty training programs with workbooks and practical solutions to organizational problems. Andrew conducts over one hundred and fifty training programs annually and maintains a private practice in hypnotherapy. He founded the Training Consortium‡, a national network and referral service that matches trainers with organizations. Andrew is the author of *Delegating Authority*, published by Barron's Educational Services, July 1992. He has written over one hundred training and development articles. His upcoming books include *Time Management, Training for Trainers,* and *Performance Management.* He is also the coauthor of AMACOM's "Creative Problem Solving and Decision Making" tape series. Andrew's professional background includes extensive research in human consciousness. He has held positions as director of Equinnox Holistic Health & Arts Center, manager of training (information services) at the Massachusetts Institute of Technology, director of education and training for Camp Fire, Inc., senior trainer and training coordinator for The Management Training Program, and has worked in numerous positions at college and university counseling centers. His educational background includes a masters in counseling psychology from Boston College, a bachelors degree in psychology from the University of Vermont, and a bachelors degree in religion and philosophy from Ithaca College.

About the photographer

Darcy Dziedzic is a Boston based free-lance photographer with an extensive background in the fine arts. After receiving her BA/BS from the University of Connecticut, she continued her studies at the School of the Museum of Fine Arts in Boston. In addition to regular appearances in Boston publications, her work has been shown in the Boston Film Festival, RIT's (Rochester Institute of Technology) Under Glass Media Festival, The American Film Institute/Sony Visions tour, and the Boston Museum of Fine Arts annual showings.

Acknowledgments

I am indebted to many people; especially to the research-
ers charting this realm, to the professionals applying
these critical approaches to enhance the quality of life for
those whom they touch, and to anyone who ventures into
this domain.

Contents

Relationship-directed images

Appendix

Preface

You are about to embark upon a journey. It will not be a physical voyage; instead, you will travel both new and familiar terrains of your own creation through the use of guided imagery.

Perhaps you think you have no aptitude for visualizing. "I can't do this," you tell yourself; "I have no imagination." But visualization requires no special ability; we all visualize in our daily lives. In this book you will have the opportunity to develop these natural abilities. Exercises in guided imagery may enable you to increase your physical, emotional, and intellectual self-awareness.

Since we speak of images, we can see this journey as a backpacking trip through a mountain range. Before you start your trip, when you stand at the foot of a mountain, everything above you looks immense, distant, and unfamiliar. On the other hand, the objects in your immediate vicinity, though smaller by comparison, are distinct and familiar. They are comfortable because you know them.

If you choose to climb the mountain, however, your view of the surroundings changes. Formerly distant trees and rocks stand out along the way, and you gain a new perspective on the familiar objects you have left below. When you reach the top, you take in the entire expanse and notice that the once familiar boulders down at the bottom now hardly seem worth a second glance, and a river has become a modest stream.

On your visual-imagery hike, you may develop the same sort of global perspective. The exercises may stimulate you to see and appreciate areas of your life that have been taken for granted. Desires or responsibilities that seemed pressing may become less critical in the adjusted scheme of things. A renewed perspective is not the only reward of this expedition. You may also sharpen your ability to perceive and make choices. As a hike helps develop your body and enhance your appreciation of nature, this book will heighten your ability to create images and benefit from your journey within them.

How to use this book

Inquire Within was developed for people interested in probing specific issues in their lives as well as for those simply seeking a road map to personal growth.

Instructors can use exercises from this book in their training programs and workshops. Psychologists and counselors can use the images to relax their clients and enable them to focus more clearly on the issues at hand. Individuals currently in therapy may wish to take this book to their therapists and work on the exercises under their guidance. And people who want to understand themselves better or just be involved in the wonderful world of imagery will find this book an excellent resource for self-discovery.

Getting started

It is always tempting when faced with a new experience to jump right in and try it, but the impulsive approach will not work well here. Working with imagery takes time and practice, and learning to become relaxed is an absolute prerequisite for making this book work for you. Be sure to read through the **Learning to relax** section before going on to the imagery exercises. In this section, you will find a variety of techniques for relaxation, including some introductory visualizations. You will probably find that one or two of these techniques work better for you, and when you become familiar enough with these you can practice relaxation anywhere—without the book to guide you.

The imagery exercises have been grouped into three general sections—outer-, inner-, and relationship-directed images. Each section starts with simple exercises and progresses to more difficult ones. Although these divisions signify a particular focus, you can use the exercises in any order you wish. Just read the descriptions on the divider pages of each section and choose the exercises that interest you most.

If you have little experience with guided imagery, practice the visualization relaxation techniques in the

Learning to Relax section and then go on to the *Imagine Yourself As . . .* exercise on page 78. After you've introduced yourself to relaxation and simple imagery, there is no need to follow the images consecutively. The only prerequisite is to maintain a positive attitude toward your innate abilities. If you have doubts about your innate creativity or ability to visualize, this book will help you overcome them. By remaining open to possibilities, you may rediscover talents and abilities that you haven't been in touch with since childhood.

The exercises are not structured to take you through a step by step progression from point *A* to goal *Z* but act as companions on a journey whose direction and distance you alone will choose. You can explore stories that have a basic scenario or plot into which you supply the dialogue and supporting characters. These *stories* are like the first chapter of a book in which you become the main character. Instead of experiencing them passively, you become an active mental participant. The story may be written to lead you to question your assumptions, as an exercise in creative enrichment, or to help you get in touch—or back in touch with emotions surrounding your individual, private experiences. Sometimes a guided image is tailored to widen your experience and increase self-confidence. The images themselves are deliberately rich and open-ended, so the same exercise can be used for many different purposes as you change and grow. Used effectively, these exercises will create new experiences on which the conscious and subconscious minds can collaborate to effect positive change.

This book provides you with a new way to view the garden of the subconscious. Unlike those situations where you try to reason with your emotions, with guided imagery you do not judge, you observe. You see the earlier memories, the experiences, the *images* as they are inside—to find out which seeds are in there and how deeply they're rooted.

The imagery exercises that follow will strengthen your mental and emotional muscles and suggest new approaches to issues you face. They will make you more conscious of the assumptions you make about yourself and the people with whom you interact. No matter where you are in life or how familiar you become with guided imagery, you can employ its principles and exercises again and again for new insight and added perspective.

Following each exercise are process questions to help you reflect on your experience. Most self-exploratory books do not provide debriefings and follow-ups. As a result, people have a tendency not to assess what they've experienced. They merely go for the ride and move on. Although the richness of imagery can be a creative end in itself, each individual reacts uniquely to the exercises— sometimes startlingly so. Taking the time to read and answer the questions may help you view your experience from a different angle or illuminate a portion of the image that you have difficulty approaching.

If you who wish to learn more about guided imagery—its historical background and relationship to the subconscious—you will find two informative essays in the appendix of this book. The history and background pages provide the context and support for what you are about to do and where you are about to venture.

The relaxation environment

To relax properly and use the imagery exercises effectively, create an environment conducive to imagery work. Find the right time and place to relax so you will not be disturbed. Twenty to thirty minutes of quiet, uninterrupted time works fine for becoming relaxed, but figure on spending an hour if you perform an imagery exercise afterwards.

Some people find pleasant smells and soft music relaxing. Gentle instrumental music can calm you and block out other distracting noises. If music distracts you, but you cannot tolerate total silence, a fan or a metronome will supply steady background white noise. Or you can acquire recordings created from or mimicking natural background noises—the sound of the surf, a quiet forest, or a gentle rain shower.

Colors can also affect mood and tension. Reds, for example, are stimulating and exciting. They are good to have around to counteract depression, or for courage and strength. Orange and yellow tend to be inspiring and illuminating. They evoke warmth and sunshine. Grass greens are restful and quietly invigorating. Blues and shades in the violet spectrum are particularly good for anxious or nervous times. They are perceived as cool colors that calm and soothe.

Being physically comfortable is as important as creating a good relaxation environment. Avoid using these exercises after a full meal. External comfort is as important as internal. Wear loose, comfortable clothing and remove your shoes, eyeglasses, and jewelry so you will have no unnecessary weight or pressure on your body. If you wear contact lenses, you may wish to remove them as well.

Imagery exercises are best done while sitting or lying comfortably. You want to be in a position in which you will not be tempted to fidget or shift frequently. If you choose to be seated, find a tall, straight-backed chair and sit so your back is straight and your feet are touching the ground. Keep the small of your back flush against the chair's back. Bend your knees so that your shins and thighs form a ninety-degree angle. Keep your legs uncrossed. Imagine that your spine is like a lightning rod, straight and sturdy with your center of gravity firm and your balance centered. Rest your arms at your sides, on the arms of the chair, on your thighs, or uncrossed in your lap.

Lying down on a firm surface with a pillow under your head is probably the most comfortable way to relax. If you choose to lie down, try placing your arms parallel to the sides of your body, at a ninety-degree angle from it, or straight above your head. Avoid crossing your legs or arms or resting your arms on your body. You may also place your hands under your head or bend your knees if you find that is comfortable.

Feeling relaxed

Now that you know where, when, and how to relax, how do you know when you are relaxed? This is not as self-evident as it may seem. During deep relaxation your heart and brain waves slow down, but most of us don't have the opportunity to sit behind a biofeedback machine and actually see the electronic evidence that this has happened. Fortunately, there are other signs. Some of these physical signs include fluttering eyelids, a sensation of warmth, and a tingly sensation in your hands and feet. When deeply relaxed, you may lose your spatial awareness and your sense of the passage of time. An hour may seem like a few minutes, and vice versa.

Most people feel either light and weightless, as if they were floating into space, or soft and heavy, as if they were sinking into warm sand at the beach. Lightness or heaviness are major indicators that your body is deeply relaxed.

When you emerge from your relaxation, you might feel slightly groggy, or a little dizzy or disoriented. This is particularly likely if you come out of a relaxed state too quickly. If this happens to you, get some fresh air, splash cold water on your face, or go back into a lightly relaxed state and prepare to reawaken feeling alert and fresh.

As your comfort and familiarity with relaxation grows, you can learn to relax in almost any setting whenever you wish to slow down and reorder your thinking. Some people, for instance, take advantage of the time they spend on buses and trains by simply closing their eyes and concentrating on their inner relaxation.

How to use the imagery exercises

With practice, you can develop a greater facility for creating images. In the beginning, however, do not be surprised if some images are difficult to visualize, or if you seem to see something but cannot interact easily with it. Most of us depend heavily on sight, filing in the background the important messages we receive from our other inputs. It can take some time and experimentation to bring the sounds and tastes clearly into focus. Some people find it helpful to link smells and textures to visual experiences. Most of us, for example, can re-create the taste or smell of popcorn when we visualize a movie theatre. As time progresses, these linkages will strengthen the visualizations.

Taping the exercises

The imagery exercises often ask you to close your eyes and visualize, which is problematic to say the least when you have to read. Reading the text while doing an imagery exercise forces you to divide your energy and attention between the mechanics of sight reading or memorization and the free flight of mental imagery.

Clearly, the best way to experience guided imagery is to close your eyes, listen to the image unfold, and follow the suggestions in the exercise. If you prefer to work alone, to preserve the privacy and anonymity this book offers, tape recording the exercises that most interest you allows you to listen passively without worrying about memorization or reading.

When taping an exercise, avoid recording any distracting background noises. Speak calmly, slowly, and expressively, and make sure you do what the exercise says. If an exercise, for example, tells you to pause or to visualize something, allow enough time for that on the tape. The key to working with these images involves going slowly enough for integration and the exploration of any important insights or feelings.

You can also ask someone to tape record images for you, or you may want someone to read the exercises to you; someone who knows you well enough to see when to speed up, slow down, or pause. Working with someone else leads to opportunities for conversation, sharing, intimacy, and mutual growth. But it is important that you trust and feel comfortable with this person. Be clear on how active or passive a role you want him or her to play.

Any reactions your narrator may have to the images should be addressed after the exercise has been completed. However, if you or your narrator approach an image that is too emotionally charged, either of you should be able to say, "Stop" or "Are you OK?"

In conclusion

Imagery is generally a safe process. Your subconscious is well defended, and in almost every case will force you to break concentration on an image if it becomes threatening.

If you begin to feel stress or intense discomfort in experiencing an image, return to the point at which you began to undergo it and back off. These images are referred to as *exercises* for good reason. Just as an athlete beginning to feel discomfort or resistance will slow down and stretch the tight muscle, so should you. Approach the point of tension slowly and stretch a bit further each time until you are comfortable experiencing it.

Sometimes you may get stuck on a specific image exercise, even after you have attained a reasonable facility in mental imagery. You may have trouble creating the image, or sustaining it, or the images that surface may seem totally unrelated to what seems to be the subject of the exercise. If this happens, first read and try to answer the process questions at the end of the image. Then leave the image for a few days or weeks, and return to it fresh. In many cases, the block will be gone. If the situation persists, or the image is troubling, you might seek out a qualified professional who can work on it with you.

A note to professionals

If you are a counselor, psychologist, or workshop leader and plan on using this book with your clients, you will need to provide an environment that is comfortable and free of distractions. You may also wish to have some type of relaxing music on hand. Before you read any script, let your listeners know that they do not have to participate in any image that they find troubling. They are in control and can stop the imaging process at any time they choose.

The relaxation and imagery scripts contained in this book are not intended to provide or be a substitute for medical or psychological advice on personal health matters. If this assistance is needed, consult a physician, therapist, or other health care professional. Neither the author nor Whole Person Associates assumes responsibility for the improper use of the exercises in this book.

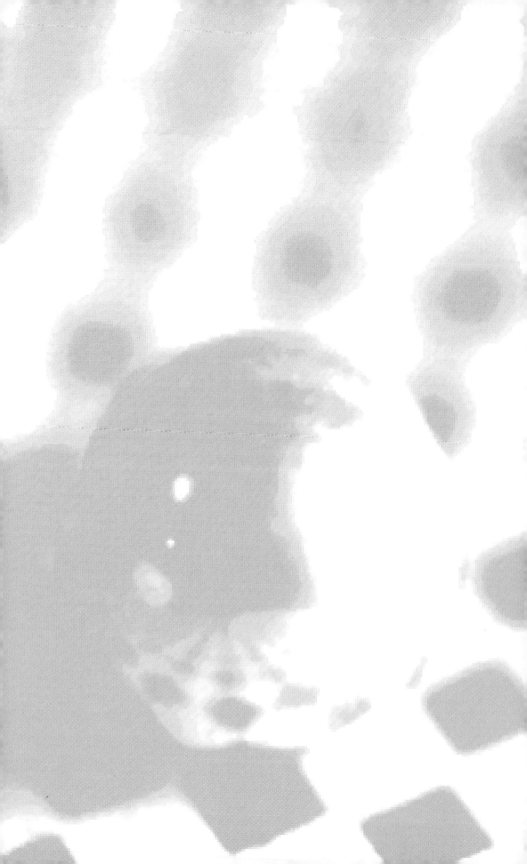

Learning to relax: preparation/practice

Relaxing properly prepares you to fully experience the imagery exercises and helps you stay healthy and sane in your everyday life. The stress-reducing techniques in this section are not difficult to do, and you should familiarize yourself with them before performing an imagery exercise.

Although the relaxation methods in this section have proven successful for many people, they do not cover all the possible ways of relaxing and preparing to create images. Be aware, however, that simply taking a few deep breaths and going on with your day does not help you relax sufficiently. Any true form of relaxation requires breathing deeply from your diaphragm (not just from the upper part of your lungs), clearing your mind of worries, and consciously addressing muscular tension.

On page 30, you will find a progressive relaxation exercise that incorporates many of the techniques from this section. This exercise provides a strong foundation on which to build your particular relaxation approach, and you can modify it, using any of the relaxation techniques you choose.

Relaxing properly takes practice, and the techniques in this section will help you start. Try them out and discover which work best for you.

Physical relaxation techniques

Most of us have experienced releasing muscle tension through walking, dancing, or sports. Stress-reducing activity, however, does not have to be strenuous. The techniques listed below provide safe and less strenuous ways to stimulate your nerves, increase blood flow, and relax your body.

Head tapping. Using your fingertips, tap lightly and quickly all over your head, starting in the back and moving around the ears to the sides. Then gently tap your forehead and the entire facial area.

Head slapping. Allow your hands to take the shape of your head and keep your wrists loose. Don't hold your breath while slapping, but continue to breathe normally. When using both hands, slap simultaneously to avoid jarring. Use a bouncing motion and slap the back of your head. Move down to the back of your neck. Now slap around the sides and over the forehead. Repeatedly slap any area that you feel needs more attention.

Face slapping. Close your eyes. With your eyes still closed, begin tapping your forehead with your fingers. Hold your hands semi-flat and have them strike simultaneously so there is no jarring. Next, move to your jaw and slap vigorously, using palms as well as fingers. Then move gently over your nose and just use fingertips over your eyelids. Finally, lower your hands.

Arm slapping. Close your eyes and focus your attention on your arms. Think about how they feel. Then open your eyes and extend your left arm in front of you at shoulder level. With your right hand slap both the top and bottom sides of your left arm from shoulder to fingertips. Repeat several times, up and down both sides of your arm. Next, bend your left elbow so that your arm is at right angles to your left shoulder. Shake your arm for fifteen seconds, allowing your left hand to wave back and forth freely. Slowly let your arm drift down to your side. Close your eyes and experience the arm you have worked on. After a sufficient break, do the same with your right arm.

Chest-slapping and yelling. This exercise may remind you of Tarzan calling in the jungle for Jane. Slap the entire area of your chest, holding your palms and fingers flat. As with the other exercises, apply some force but remain gentle. As you continue slapping, move back toward the armpits, above the breasts, and make the sound "AHHHHH," as continuously and as loudly as possible. Continue this for about 15 to 20 seconds. Then put your hands down and experience the effects. Yelling expels old air and some of the held-in feelings.

Singing. This achieves the same effect as chest-slapping and yelling.

Standing on head. If done properly with correct support, standing on your head promotes good circulation and reenergizes the body.

Relaxation enhancements

Once you have learned how to use physical relaxation techniques, you may wish to deepen their effects by using some of the methods listed below.

Counting down and progressive relaxation. This progressive relaxation exercise consists of assigning a number to each area of your body and counting down while focusing on the numbered areas. For example, in your mind you say and picture the number ten to initiate your relaxation, then you say and picture the number nine while concentrating on your toes. Continue counting down and focusing on different areas of your body until you reach zero. After practicing this technique, you may be able to achieve a tension-free state merely by counting down.

Counting alone. After you have performed some other relaxation exercise, slowly count down from 100 to 0, 50 to 0, 25 to 0, or 10 to 0 to feel the effects of this deepening exercise.

Zen counting and breathing. Breathing exercises used alone or with progressive relaxations are quite effective for achieving a state of relaxation. To perform this technique, get in a comfortable position, take a slow, deep breath, and close your eyes. Breathe out, pushing every bit of air out of your lungs. Then inhale and picture the number three while holding your breath for three seconds. Visualize the number three in any way you wish: as a white number against a black curtain, as a neon light, etc. Then exhale slowly and completely, and as you do, mentally say "three" three times. By the third "three" you will have finished your exhalation. Breathe in again and hold your breath for three seconds while seeing the number two, then exhale while holding the mental image of the number and saying "two" three times. Repeat this same process of holding and releasing your breath for three seconds while imagining the number one.

1-4 counting. This simple exercise is very powerful if done correctly. Inhale and exhale completely. Inhale again while mentally counting from one to four. Holding your breath, count again from one to four, then count from one to eight while exhaling completely. Do this exercise three times.

Section breathing. Breathe deeply while concentrating on the mechanics of how you breathe. Feel the oxygen enter and fill your lungs. See your lungs divided into three sections—bottom, middle, and top. Feel the bottom section of your lungs expand with air, then your rib cage press forward, and, finally, your shoulders rise as you complete your inhalation. Then exhale slowly and completely while lowering your shoulders. To push out the last remaining bits of air, pull in your abdomen. This exercise should be repeated four times.

Nostril breathing. To become even more aware of your breathing patterns, close off your left nostril with your left forefinger. Inhale through your right nostril and hold that breath for a count of six. Then remove your left forefinger, close off your right nostril, and exhale fully through your left nostril. Repeat this exercise ten times. This exercise may be done in various ways: single nostril breathing, alternate nostril breathing, nostril to mouth breathing, and nostril breathing alone.

Verbal statements. Give yourself a series of positive suggestions, such as "I feel calm," or "I am relaxed," as you breathe and relax. Know that every word you think has an effect on your body.

Mantra/Chants. Repeat any word, number, or phrase while you are relaxing. Repetition focuses one's concentration and helps facilitate relaxation.

Metronome. Listen to the repetition of a metronome at approximately 76 beats per minute (the average heart rate for humans), while saying "Re" to yourself as you breathe in, and "lax" as you breathe out.

Eye-fixation. Staring at any object—a candle, a crystal, or a spot on the wall—can relax you. Place the object one to two feet from you at eye level. Be sure that no other objects compete for your attention. Stare at the object until your eyes get heavy or drowsy and you feel like closing them. You can vary this method by staring at an object above your forehead, one to three feet in front of you.

Visualization relaxation techniques

Your body has the ability to react to mental pictures as if they were real. The following visualization exercises help you relax by having you imagine yourself in various settings, as yourself or as inanimate objects, engaged in relaxing activities. These exercises not only help you relax but also provide a solid introduction to the value and power of guided imagery.

Bubbles. Imagine that your thoughts are bubbles, which float up and out of you, clearing your mind as they go. Or picture bubbles rising to the surface of a glass of soda water. As the carbonated bubbles reach the surface and burst, release any thoughts you may have with them. Clear your mind and continue watching the glass. As each bubble reaches the surface, relate it to the letting go of your own bubbling tension. Continue to release your tensions as you watch all the bubbles escape, until you have relaxed your mind and body and the glass of carbonated water is crystal clear and undisturbed.

Escalator. Imagine stepping onto the top of a long, slow-moving escalator. While you slowly ride down this escalator, feel yourself going down, down, down into a deeper and deeper state of relaxation. Allow your entire body to relax as you continue to ride down this escalator.

Elevator. Picture yourself about to enter an elevator on the tenth floor of an office building. The doors open and you enter. You press the button for the ground floor. As the elevator travels downward, let out a deep breath with each floor that you pass and feel your body relaxing. When you reach the ground level, step out into any place you choose.

Staircase. For a similar effect to that of riding the elevator or escalator, imagine walking down a spiral staircase or striding down a wide, cool mountain path.

Hammock. For those who do not get motion sickness, this image can be fun and effective. Imagine yourself as a hammock, gently swaying back and forth in a light breeze. Feel your weightlessness and relax. If you have difficulty visualizing yourself as a hammock, then imagine you are in a hammock, which gradually drops away, leaving just you swaying in the breeze.

Switchboard. For those who enjoy working with machines or computers, this image may come easily. Imagine yourself as a huge switchboard with lights that monitor each part of your body as it relaxes. You can see lights switch on or watch different colors light up as you relax. Take the time to feel yourself relax.

Floating clouds. Explore a feeling of airiness and lightness with this image. Close your eyes and picture a bright, sunny day. The air is still except for a few wispy clouds that glide by. Imagine yourself as one of those white, fluffy clouds. Feel the sensation of weightlessness as you allow yourself to drift through the sky. You feel warmed by the sun, and very buoyant. If you have any difficulty with this image, you may first want to visualize yourself in an airplane. Gaze out of your window and see the sea of cotton clouds below you. Imagine yourself safely stepping out of the plane and onto the clouds. You bounce from one mound to another until you land on the one you will become. Imagine lying down on this cloud bed, then allow yourself to become the floating cloud.

Bird on a wind current. Imagine yourself on a ship on a clear, bright day. You walk to the rear of the deck and see a row of sea gulls, swept up in the wind currents. They appear to be motionless, but you know that they are following the ship. Watch how peacefully they glide up and down, as if they were pulled by strings. Then relax and imagine you are a gull in that air current. Feel the sensation of warmth and weightlessness as you look down at the sparkling sea. You can move wherever you wish to go with little effort. Your wings are outspread and your feathers tingle from the mist of the sea. Enjoy this relaxing journey.

Hot air balloon. Picture yourself as a colorful inflatable balloon. Mentally inflate yourself with every inhalation. Imagine yourself gently rising to the ceiling, or if outdoors, to the sky. Take in the scenery around you as you gently continue to rise. Notice all the details of your surroundings: the colors, objects, smells, temperature, and so on. You can float as long as you wish, and when you are ready to return, slowly exhale. With each exhalation, gently return to your original position. Take time to enjoy this feeling.

Smoke rings. Another "floating in space" sensation can be achieved with this image. Once you are relaxed, visualize smoke rings that slowly rise from a fire. Picture the concentric circles getting wider and wider as they continue to rise into the air. Imagine the smoke rings enveloping you, until you become the airy rings spiraling upward into space. As with similar images, you can drift wherever you want, for as long as you choose. Have fun and be creative.

Space travel. You may want to initiate this exercise by staring up at a starlit night. Then, find a comfortable position, relax, and envision the stars. Imagine you have a zoom camera lens or telescope and are able to get a very close look at the glittering points and fireballs. When you are calm and relaxed, deepen this state by seeing yourself as an object traveling in space. Picture and feel yourself drifting weightlessly and effortlessly through the blackness. See the deep blue-black color of the universe all around you. Watch stars and planets slowly recede as you move past them and continue further into space. As you see each star recede, you will become more and more relaxed, in a deeper and deeper state of mind. Now visualize an area of fuzzy white light in front of you. See yourself travel closer and closer to this brightness until you feel yourself bathed by its warmth and can feel the energy. Travel into the center of the light. In this light, you feel clean and open. Stay in the light as long as you need to, and when you are ready, slowly return to earth.

Magic carpet. Another way to achieve the floating sensation involves imagining yourself as a magic carpet, flying away from daily activities and pressures. Get into a comfortable position, close your eyes, and relax. Picture yourself outdoors on a calm spring day. You are tempted to lie down in the cool green grass, and you do so. Now picture a comfortable, lightweight carpet made of any material and any color you want. Imagine lying on this carpet, sinking more and more into it until you become the very fibers in the material. Feel yourself, your limbs, spreading out, and when you are ready, take a deep breath and take off. You can control your speed and location. Your travel will be effortless and you will always be in control. You will have no distractions or demands made on you. Enjoy the sensation of complete serenity and freedom as you view the sights below. When you are ready, lower yourself to the ground, gently and slowly, and savor your experience.

Ice cube. This image emphasizes the melting action of an ice cube, not its coolness. Imagine yourself as an ice cube, resting in a very comfortable place. You are not cold. Feel your edges soften and relax. Watch the melted water slide off and away, and feel your hard body melting away into water. Let your body melt into total relaxation.

Progressive relaxation exercise

Progressive relaxation can take an active or a passive form. In an active approach you tense your muscles before relaxing them. In a passive one you concentrate on relaxing your muscles without tightening them first. Some people find that active progressive relaxation actually increases their tension, so this exercise, which combines other techniques and ideas from this section, takes the passive route. Since your muscles are never tensed intentionally, they should remain unstressed at all times.

Experiment with this exercise, modifying it in any manner you choose, until you find a method for relaxing that works best for you. Then go on to the imagery exercises that follow.

Preparation
Get in a comfortable position. Take a few deep breaths and exhale fully, allowing yourself to relax. With each exhalation let all the daily concerns leave your mind.

Exercise
Become aware of how your skin feels against the surface on which you are lying or sitting. Feel your body supported and allow yourself to settle in.

Now take a deep breath and focus completely on your feet. Allow your feet to let go of tension. Be aware of how you feel as this happens and savor any of the good feelings you are experiencing.

Now focus your attention on your lower legs, noticing how they feel. Take a deep breath while concentrating all your energy on your lower legs. As you exhale, release all the tension you are holding there.

Shift now to your thighs and knees. Become aware of how they feel—notice the air around them. Take note of any tension you may feel as you take a deep breath. And as you exhale, release this tension. Your knees and legs are now totally relaxed. Enjoy the feeling.

Now focus on your hips and buttocks. Become aware of how they feel resting against the surface you are on. Focus on any tension in these areas as you take a deep breath. As you exhale, send away all the tension from these areas.

Draw your attention to your abdomen. Notice how this area feels and detect any tension. Take another deep breath, focusing on any tension, and release it as you exhale. Take another deep breath, allowing the air to completely oxygenate your abdomen. As you exhale, dispel any excess tension with the air you breathe out.

Next consider your chest and diaphragm. You may find that you are storing extra tension there, which inhibits your ability to take full and complete breaths. Now you can allow those areas to become free of all tension and to relax completely. Take a deep breath, and let every bit of tension flow from your body with your exhalation.

Focus your attention on any stress in your back, neck, and head. Stay aware of this tension while taking a slow, deep breath. As you exhale, release all the tension and imagine it flowing out and away from you. Continue exhaling and releasing tension until this area feels completely relaxed and loose. Feel your head getting heavy and sinking into the surface that supports it.

Progressive relaxation

Now focus once again on your legs—from your hips to your feet. By now they should be feeling relaxed and heavy. Focus on any remaining tension, inhale, and with a deep exhalation, release any residue stress.

You are now ready to shift your attention to your lower back. Focus on any tension that might exist in this area, take a deep breath, and during your exhalation dismiss the excess tension in this area of your body. Concentrate on allowing your back to become completely limp and stress-free. Relax with your next exhalation, and imagine releasing as much of the built-up tension as you can at this time. Allow yourself to let go and release any tensions that may have accumulated in your back.

Imagine a small sun helping you to relax as it rises up your back like dawn breaking on a warm summer day. As it rises, imagine this sun's rays spreading out over your entire back and, like fingers of warmth, massaging away, melting away, dissipating any tension. Allow this sun to rise slowly, relaxing your entire back until the sun lifts off of your head. As it rises into the sky, it will take with it any excess tension that remains.

As the sun continues to rise, shift your attention to your mouth and jaw and notice how they feel. Notice whether you are clenching your jaw or biting your lip. Know that with your next deep breath you will alleviate any tension you feel here.

Now inhale, focusing on any tension, and then exhale, releasing all the stored energy and stress. Take another deep breath, focusing on any remaining stress, and with your exhalation, let go of as much tension as you can. Continue to breathe in, let go, and relax.

Turn your attention to your forehead and eyes. Become aware of any tightness. Inhale slowly and deeply, and when you exhale, feel the tension leave your body like rising steam. Take another deep breath, and as you exhale, allow any residual tension to flow through and out of your body. Take a moment to enjoy how completely relaxed your eyes and forehead feel, and how you continue to completely relax.

While the sun moves up and out of sight, prepare to take three very deep breaths. Focus on any tension in the neck, head, and face. Know how they feel, and then with each exhalation, free all of the tension and allow relaxation to enter.

Now focus on your shoulders and upper arms. Inhale and concentrate on any tension you may be keeping there. Knowing that you can release it, take a deep breath, and with the next exhalation, completely allow the tension to leave these areas.

Become aware of your lower arms and hands, and with your next inhalation, notice any tension stored there. And when you exhale, allow all the tensions to float from your arms and hands, letting these limbs become limp and relaxed. Allow your arms to feel heavy and relaxed, sinking into the surface they rest on.

As your entire body continues to relax, take a deep, enjoyable breath, feeling the sensation of total relaxation throughout your entire body, from your feet to your head. Appreciate the feeling of relaxation and once again check your body to locate any tension.

Concentrate on any stressful area, take a deep breath, and imagine the air traveling right into this area. As you exhale, imagine this area relaxing and the tension traveling out. Repeat this action as often as necessary.

As you continue to relax, picture yourself in this tranquil state. Take note of how your body feels and hold onto this image of yourself for a reference point in the future. Whenever you discover tension within yourself, remember what relaxation feels like and move into that memory. Once you have mastered it, you can teach yourself to relax at anytime.

In a moment, it will be time to come back to a state of full awareness, but you do not have to lose this feeling of relaxation. You may bring it back with you to a waking state. Now, take one more deep breath, and as you exhale open your eyes. Slowly stretch, and begin to move your limbs, returning to a completely awakened state while remaining relaxed.

Outer-directed images

The exercises in this section help you examine how your actions impact and influence the world and how outer influences affect your inner reality. Each image allows you to go beyond your physical self to work with your perceptions and reactions, observations and judgments, as well as experiences and expectations.

learning experiences. In this exercise, you will close off your sense of sight so you can learn to rely more on other senses and inner resources.

Tropical paradise

This exercise will enable you to create the most wonderful place in the world—a place where you can experience the sensations of total comfort, clarity of mind, and relaxation. In this place of beauty you can enjoy life and adopt an attitude toward it that is open, exploratory, self-paced, and revitalizing. Through the experience of this idyllic "vacation" you may develop a calmness and clarity that you can use to revitalize your daily routine.

Work

In this exercise, you can learn to "go on vacation" at work by approaching it from a positive, relaxed, well-centered state. You will see yourself in a stressful work situation and envision changes in your approach to it rather than trying to change the situation or the other people involved.

Mishaps

Little moments of stress can throw us in different ways. Depending on our character and the situation, we can either forget a mishap or let it wreck our whole day. Usually, we can laugh about it after enough time has passed, or if we see it happen to someone else. This exercise, which allows you to observe someone else suffer a series of mishaps, should provide some comic relief and may help you prepare for mishaps that happen to you.

Cube on
the screen

This exercise asks you to imagine a simple object and impose changes upon it. Choose your own speed; take as long as you need for each adjustment.

Note: Some people have an easier time with certain colors and shapes. You may want to practice this exercise until all the transformations become smooth and easy.

Preparation
Sit in a comfortable chair and take three deep breaths. On your last exhale, imagine a white projection screen in front of you.

Exercise
Your white projection screen stands before you, and you will be the projector.

First, project a circle on the screen. Draw it and adjust it until it is perfectly round. Study its shape; note the size and curvature.

Now fill the interior of the circle with the color blue. Study the result: a blue circle. Once you clearly see the blue circle on the white screen, change it to red. Fill in all the space within its boundary until you have a red circle. Study it until you have it clearly before you.

Now, instead of changing the color, you are going to change the shape. Keeping the same red hue, change the circle into a triangle of comparable size. Now you should have a red triangle on a white screen. Once the red triangle is clearly visible, change it to blue. Study the blue triangle on the white screen.

Now you are going to change the shape of the blue triangle. Adjust its shape from three to four equal sides so that it becomes a blue square on the white screen. Study the blue square until you are satisfied that it is complete and solid. Now change it to a red square. Fill the interior until it is completely red. You now have a red square in front of you.

As soon as the red square is clear to you, change it back to a red circle. Then reach out with your hand and pull the red circle off the screen. As you pull, the circle stretches out and becomes a sphere. By the time it is fully in your hand it resembles a miniature red sun the size of a light bulb.

Study the red sphere in your hand. Note its texture with your eyes and fingers. Feel its weight in your palm. Once you see and feel the red sphere completely— change its color to blue. You now hold a blue sphere in your hand. Its weight and texture remain the same.

Now change the shape from a blue sphere to a blue pyramid of comparable size. Study the shape, edges, texture, color—its reality. After you have fully studied the blue pyramid, adjust its color to red. You now have a red pyramid to hold and examine. Study the red pyramid fully.

Now the red pyramid is about to become a red cube.

Make it a red cube and study your handiwork. You are now holding a red cube. Turn it over, study its six faces, its size, shape, weight, and texture. Allow yourself to become comfortable with this red cube. Then, when you are ready, change its color to blue. In your hand you are holding a blue cube.

Once you have sufficiently studied this blue cube, you are ready to return the object to the screen. Place it on the white screen in whatever form you choose. Once it is there, roll up the screen. Breathe easily, count to three, and open your eyes, calmly reflecting on the experience. One . . . Two . . . Three.

Questions for reflection

Which transformations were easiest for you?

Which were the most difficult?

Which particular shape and color combinations seemed to give you more pleasure?

Did any other senses come into play? Did you associate heat, coolness, textures, or aromas with certain transformations?

Some readers new to imagery may doubt their ability to visualize. They may doubt the power of imagery to elicit physical and emotional responses in themselves. Here is a simple exercise that illustrates imagery's power and the ease in which you can call it into play.

Preparation

Sitting comfortably in a kitchen may help you experience this image more effectively. Place an orange on the table. While focusing on it, feel your eyelids getting heavy. Take three deep breaths and with your third exhalation, let your eyes close.

Making juice

Exercise

Imagine that it is morning. You have just risen from bed, and you go to the kitchen to make some fresh orange juice.

You open the refrigerator and look in the bottom drawer. Nestled inside are two fresh, plump oranges. Pick them up and place them on the counter. Locate a wooden cutting board, a knife, and a large glass, and place them beside the oranges.

With care, pick up the first orange and prepare to slice it in half. As you watch the knife gently saw through the spongy skin, a light fog of spray fills the air above the

cutting board and settles on your hands like dew.
Putting the two halves at one end of the board, you pick
up the second orange. Again the shiny blade slices into
the soft orange peel and the bright spray cools your
hands and darkens the cutting board.

Now you have four shiny, dripping orange halves on
the board. Not only does moisture from the orange
halves drip to the board, but the cold skin perspires
with condensed water from the air.

Pick up one half and hold it over the glass. Then
squeeze, watching the liquid stream out. As it slows to
a quick dripping, tighten your grip. Sweet, wonderful
juice accumulates in the glass as you grind the orange
half to the pulp.

Tossing the empty skin aside, you pick up the second
orange half. As you squeeze it, you notice pale bits of
pulp plop into the glass. Once half of the glass has
turned bright orange with succulent juice, add the third
orange half.

Your hands are now cool, wet, and sticky from the
refreshing liquid. Squeezing again, you send another
small torrent into the glass. The juice is almost ready.

You pick up the last half and squeeze, filling the glass
almost to the brim. With a little extra pressure, you
force out a few last delicate drops of orange nectar.
Then you toss aside the skin. Before you stands a tall,
refreshing glass of fresh-squeezed orange juice.

Questions for reflection

Were you able to imagine every step of this image clearly?

Were there any points where you had difficulty?

Did other senses besides sight come into play? Could you feel, taste, or smell anything?

As you thought about making orange juice, what happened?

Taking a hot bath, getting a massage, exercising, sipping a cool drink—there are many ways to relax. Here is a method for relaxing that involves creating the rhythmic, physical sensation of sitting in a rocking chair.

Preparation

Sit in a comfortable chair that rests solidly on the floor, take three deep breaths, and relax.

Rocking chair

Exercise

You are going to imagine that you are sitting in a rocking chair. First, allow yourself to relax, and focus your awareness on your breathing. The air rushes in and rushes out. Your ribs rise, then fall.

As you inhale, your body seems to open up, rise, and push up your head. As you breathe out, your body contracts again, and your head falls downward. Your body has its own rocking motion.

As time passes, allow yourself to close your eyes. You may gradually feel the chair begin to rock. The chair is rocking with the motion of your body.

Focus on the rocking motion. Encourage your body to

contribute to the motion. Don't push or strain, but add a little energy to the rocking chair to sustain its gentle swaying.

As the chair rocks back and forth, note how this rocking motion relaxes you. Its repetition is like rolling waves, swaying trees, and other natural motions. The rocking motion goes on and on, and you become more and more relaxed.

Eventually the rocking motion begins to slow down. You are no longer concentrating your energy on the rocker's motion. The chair is merely rocking with the energy of its momentum; not pushing, not straining, but relaxing. Try to remain aware of your feelings as the rocking chair slows down.

The chair's motion becomes gentler and gentler. The arc of its swaying is small, but it is still moving. It is moving your body only slightly.

You are slowing down completely. Finally the rocker comes to a stop. Take a moment to explore all your feelings. Notice the total absence of motion.

Relax. Take three deep breaths and on your third exhalation, open your eyes. Once your eyes are open, realize that you are no longer sitting in the imaginary rocking chair.

Take a moment to note your surroundings and feel the solidity of your chair standing on the floor.

Questions for reflection

What were the different motions you noticed in your breathing? Were you surprised by their complexity and the rocking of your body?

How soon did you feel the chair begin to rock? Was this a surprise?

Did the rocking remind you of other motions?

Was there anything disturbing about the rocking motion?

How did you feel as the rocking slowed and stopped?

Most of us have experienced physical exhaustion, whether from shoveling snow, putting in long hours at the office, or playing in a sport. Sometimes we have chosen or been forced by the situation to push further than we expected, and we have found a second wind—extra energy and exhilaration that carried us beyond our old limits. This can happen in a relationship as well as in physical exercise.

In this image you will experience a physical activity to the point of fatigue, then you will push beyond it. Whether you have actually done this before or not, this mental exercise may teach you something about endurance and give you a greater appreciation of your body.

Physical exercise

Preparation
Decide whether you want to imagine yourself swimming or running, then choose where and when you wish to swim or run. Next, physically stretch out as if you were preparing for an actual workout. As soon as you are finished, lie down and allow your mind to relax. Feel your blood surging, your body alert and alive, your mind open and ready.

Exercise
Properly dressed and finished with your stretching exercises, you are ready for your long workout. You prepare for the start and imagine hearing the pop of a starter's gun, signaling you to begin.

Physical exercise

At first you can breathe easily, with only a slight physical stiffness, a resistance in your muscles from not having done this type of exercise in a while. But for the most part, you are hardly conscious of any physical exertion. Note the swing of your arms and the sweep of your legs as you move. In your mind's eye you can see a powerful body setting off on an impressive journey.

After a minute or two, your breath has become quicker and fuller, and you adjust your pace in rhythm to your body. Feel the heat rising inside the muscles of your upper arms and thighs. Blood surges through all the vessels of your body, carrying oxygen in and waste out. Hear your blood pulse in your temples.

You are now settling into a steady rhythm. All your limbs are working in concert, carrying you forward. Muscles tense and relax, tense and relax, tense and relax. Lungs fill up like a balloon and then deflate as they push the air out.

While you are moving at this comfortable pace, take inventory of muscles that are not directly involved in this workout. Often, when people are not in shape, they may inadvertently clench their jaw as they exercise. Others hold their head stiffly on their neck or hunch their shoulders. This undesired tension wastes energy and forces your body to work against itself. Check yourself and locate any of your tension zones as you continue to work out. Allow yourself to relax these isolated areas and integrate them into your overall bodily activity.

You are at your peak of performance now. As you reach this optimum level of physical performance, it feels as though all the garbage that has built up inside your body is being cleansed and melted away. Feel yourself purified and strengthened. Even your mind is cleared of cobwebs as the blood pumps and surges through.

Many minutes have passed since you began and now the first hints of fatigue begin to show. Your rhythm starts to falter. You do not reach forward with quite as much confidence. Despite your best efforts, your neck and jaw muscles remain stiff, pulling your head from side to side.

On your right side you start to feel an ache just under the lowest rib. It is the familiar stitch that plagues athletes who are not in top shape. Grimly, you proceed at the pace you have been maintaining up until now.

Soon your mind is receiving more signals to slow down or stop. Muscles that have been working the hardest are now aching. Stiff joints unused to such continuous labor start to hurt. Feel the soreness in your shoulders and knees, as if they are rusty and not getting enough oil.

Now your mind is registering weary aches in your upper arms, stiffness in your lower back, and actual pain in your right side. Your arms are not swinging or sweeping as fully; they have been pulled in closer to your body as if to protect it. Your legs no longer move as crisply; they have begun to flail a little. Your dia-phragm pulls hard to suck sufficient air into your lungs, and you feel yourself gasping.

Overall weariness has set in. Signals to stop are coming from all over your body. Your mind feels dizzy from the load of messages and lack of oxygen. Your limbs feel heavier than usual, and you have to concentrate to keep them moving.

As you continue to move forward on some sort of desperate automatic pilot, your mind starts to drift toward daydreams of giving up. Imagine what it would feel like to stop, lie down on some grass, and relax. Your breathing would subside and your blood would be able to clean out all the waste that is weighing down your aching muscles. The pain would fade away and your mind could be at peace.

It would be so easy to stop here. Yet your arms and legs continue to propel you forward, and you wonder: *have I done all I can? Is my body really in danger, or is it merely crying out like a child? Are the pain signals honestly forecasting a physical collapse or injury, or is my body complaining simply because I rarely put such impressive demands upon it.*

Keep moving. Push on a little farther and see what happens. Swing your arms forward and pull them back like clubs: pump your legs as if the world has ended. You are no longer conscious of where you are, how fast or slow you are moving, how warm or cold your skin feels. You feel only the next stroke, the next kick, the next step, the next breath of air.

And suddenly, like sunlight breaking through the clouds, the pain and pressure recede. It's no longer a strain to get enough oxygen, and your limbs feel lighter again. Everything feels smoother, more rhythmic and limber, and you feel as though you are moving faster than you were before.

You have reached your second wind. What a great feeling it is to go beyond what you thought were your limits!

As your body continues to propel you forward, you feel you know what it was like for Roger Bannister to run the first four-minute mile or Joan Benoit to win the Olympic marathon. Perhaps you imagine you can hear the roar of a crowd and see the smiling faces of your family and friends.

It feels good to know that you have made it this far. A triumphant weariness sets in. Your mind begins to wander again, not because it is embattled and hungry for air, but because it is now safe for it to relax.

Frantic signals no longer come in from your limbs, and you feel no need to will yourself forward; you have already gone farther than you ever expected to go. You take a mental break from the compulsion to move forward and find that you almost continue on automatically. You can breathe easier now, freely and not consciously.

If you are swimming, you may decide to turn over on your back and gently float, paddling your arms through the water. You almost feel weightless, as your fingers propel you forward. You may even close your eyes and imagine the water as a huge bathtub or spring, rejuvenating and soothing your muscles.

If you are running, you slow down to a stroll—enjoying a tingling sensation all over. Whereas before you were pushing and driving, working your muscles hard, now you can freely swing your arms. You may want to stop periodically to stoop or rub your legs. When you have finished winding down, you once again revel in your accomplishment. You know that having achieved this limit and reaching your second wind enables you to return to this point at any time.

Questions for reflection

Which exercise did you choose to do and why? Was it an activity you had experienced before?

Were you able to experience the warm up in the preparation? What happened?

Did you have any difficulty isolating the tense areas while doing the activity? Were you successful in relaxing these muscles?

How soon into the activity did you feel fatigued? Did discouragement accompany this feeling? Did you feel your body ache? Did you quit or go on?

How did you feel when you got your second wind— both emotionally and physically?

Do you feel that your mental rehearsal might make you more successful at running or swimming?

Life gets difficult when our environment is disrupted or we become physically hurt. We have to tackle each situation more carefully because our usual rhythm is gone. Such difficulties, however, can be excellent learning experiences. In this exercise, you will close off your sense of sight so you can learn to rely more on other senses and inner resources.

Note: Because this exercise involves the exploration of unknown and unseen territory, try and get someone else to tape or read it to you. Its point will be lost if you know what happens before you experience it.

Fog

Preparation

Get in a comfortable seated position and, if you are outdoors, look at some clouds. If you are inside, stare at a white surface, such as a wall or refrigerator door. Study the clouds or white surface until you feel yourself relaxing, then close your eyes. Let your imagination put you on a bus.

Exercise

You are riding through town on a bus on a hot and intensely humid day. Clouds fill the sky.

Looking out the bus's window, you focus your attention on a particularly large cloud. Wisps develop at its edges and grow. This cloud expands and absorbs other smaller clouds. Slowly this huge white mass descends upon the city and envelops it. Everything fades into mist until all is dull and white.

The bus has slowed to a halt. You can tell that all other traffic has stopped because it has become very quiet outside. Everyone must be on foot now.

Before the fog descended, you knew you were not near your home or office; in fact, you were at least two miles from any familiar place. Nevertheless, you decide you would rather walk and try to find a safe refuge than wait on the crowded public vehicle. You are also a little hungry, so you head for the door.

Now you have stepped off the bus and into the white-out. Holding a hand before your face, you find that you cannot see more than three inches beyond your nose. For a moment you ponder how this makes you feel. How will you travel? Where will you go?

The unyielding whiteness closes in on you from all sides. You feel a slight panic in the heat and whiteout. Yet somehow you must get to a familiar place. You think about this and you decide to feel your way with your hands and feet. Perhaps your senses of hearing and smell will help.

With hands outstretched and feet carefully reaching forward to catch any obstructions or changes in the surface beneath you, you start to slowly walk forward. Suddenly, your hand encounters something hard and smooth. You follow it from its waist-high horizontal surface to a slippery, glassy curve and up to a second metallic plateau just below the level of your face. Your foot stubs against a surface that gives a little. You reach down to the level of your shin and feel a round object with lots of little ridges and a metal rim in the center. Of course! You have encountered a common object on the street.

Feeling your way around this recognizable object, you continue on. Your toe strikes a very hard obstacle, not very high, and you step onto it. A few steps later you encounter a wholly new obstacle.

This is a smooth wall, strictly vertical, with no curves or bumps in it. You rap your knuckle on it and hear a "clang." It is not difficult to guess what it is, but you cannot see the display behind it.

Turning away, you navigate down the sidewalk between various walls and the curb. Your hands catch an occasional lamppost or telephone pole around which you maneuver. You feel you are making excellent progress when suddenly the pavement ends! It's probably the curb, yet when you lower your foot beyond it, the drop is more than a few inches.

You explore to your right and left. On one side is a wall. On the other is a curb that you can step off of, but once again, the pavement ends in front of you.

Gingerly, you drop your foot over the side until it encounters a surface a foot and a half below. When you step down with your other leg, you find yourself on a slight incline. As you make your way down it, the earth becomes increasingly soft and moist. You take two more cautious steps and walk into a barrier that gives inward as you push at it. It is not solid, but made of smooth, narrow metallic wires that seem to be twisted together. You reach up and find a long metallic tube, and above it, the sharp ends of the twisted wires. You realize that you do not want to continue on.

Climbing back to the pavement, you step onto the sidewalk and continue down the street.

Soon you smell some delicious aromas: mustard, hot dogs, and toasted rolls. You almost run into a pushcart containing a variety of food items. The vendor is so happy to meet someone else in the fog that he offers you a free sandwich and drink. You tell him what you would like and he hands it to you.

As you eat your sandwich and drink the liquid, you feel your hunger and thirst go away. You also notice the light around you beginning to brighten. The dark shapes of nearby buildings loom and take definite form. The fog is lifting!

The bright sunny day emerges once again. As you finish your meal next to the pushcart, you glance down the street and see the construction site, the plate glass window, and the parked car you encountered in the fog. These familiar objects became mysterious obstacles that, with persistence, you identified and overcame.

In the light, you become more aware of the power of your senses, and you begin to return to your original setting, staring up at the clouds or blank wall.

Allow yourself to drift back to where you began. Slowly count to three, then open your eyes.

Questions for reflection

How did you feel when the huge cloud descended and all traffic stopped?

Was traveling without sight a new experience for you?

Aside from obstacles you encountered, did you attempt to build a mental picture of the surroundings beyond your reach?

What did you think was down the incline in the street?

How did it feel to meet the vendor in the fog?

Describe your emotions when the fog lifted and the sun appeared again.

Did the exercise suggest to you that in the past you had utilized senses other than sight far more than you knew? How easily were you able to adapt to this new environmental barrier?

Tropical paradise

In the course of the nine-to-five grind, we often feel that we are losing touch with the better parts of ourselves. We develop a constant state of tension, uneasiness, and worry. This exercise will enable you to create the most wonderful place in the world—a place where you can experience the sensations of total comfort, clarity of mind, and relaxation. In this place of beauty you can enjoy life and adopt an attitude toward it that is open, exploratory, self-paced, and revitalizing. Through the experience of this idyllic vacation you may develop a calmness and clarity that you can use to revitalize your daily routine.

Preparation

If you are not at home, imagine that you are and that you are relaxing in the comfort of your favorite room.

Exercise

As you relax in your favorite room, the mailman slips a fat envelope under the front door. You open the envelope and find the following sweepstakes notice inside:

**YOU HAVE WON
A FREE VACATION!**

Leaving at your convenience, you will travel by boat to an untouched corner of the world—your very own tropical island paradise!

Once there, you will enjoy the luxury of no watches, clocks, radios, or televisions. You will experience undisturbed isolation, lush greenery, pure air, and friendly exotic animals. All will be yours on this dream vacation!

You have been given an opportunity to leave the burden of your responsibilities at home, so see yourself boarding the boat that will take you to your island paradise.

The trip takes no time at all, and soon you see the swaying palm trees and mist-shrouded mountains of your destination.

Now you are on the beach. The sun is bright and warm, and you feel your muscles soften and relax in the sun's comforting heat. The sand beneath your bare feet is also warm, and it squishes between your toes as you walk toward the foliage. It is very peaceful here.

You are ready to enter the underbrush. As you step onto the soft moist earth of the trail, you marvel at the huge green leaves of the tropical plants and the abundant fruit and nuts growing all around you. When you run your fingers along the leaves, they feel firm and smooth to the touch. Drops of clear water collect in the hollows, run down the leaves, and hang sparkling from the edges.

Pleasant bird cries echo above you. Soon you begin to make out the shapes and fantastic colors of the birds.

Tropical paradise

Green and yellow toucans, red parrots, and birds with tufted crests and long feathered tails that hang down from their perches.

As you continue down the path, you begin to encounter friendly animals: Llamas with soft, thick fur; stylish zebras; sleepy lions; cuddly koalas; and inquisitive chimps. They do not fear you because they've never seen a human being before. You can reach out and touch them as you pass.

In the distance you can hear water. The closer you get to the brook, the more flowers of bright yellow, purple, red, blue, and white you see. Some fall from their stems as you pass, brushing your cheeks and shoulders. The mixture of fragrances fills your nostrils. You feel a warm sense of confidence, the power of your self stretching outward in response to the setting.

Now you have arrived at the brook. Just upstream is a waterfall. Water cascades down in shifting white curtains, sending up a mist that catches the sunlight in a little rainbow. From there the water laps down over stones and into the stream. Staring at the waterfall you sense the force of the spray pounding the rocks and you understand the beauty that blossoms from its strength.

A stone path follows the water. Walking downstream you notice that many bright flowers have fallen into the brook, and you travel with them. Soon you arrive at a large pool surrounded on all sides by a bed of moss.

You sit down on the moss and gaze at the clear water of the pool and the blossoms swirling lazily on its surface. The feeling of relaxation and comfort grows. Staring into the depths, you can see that only a few feet below the surface a large round passageway leads into the rock at the bottom.

You dive in and swim through the opening. Once on the other side, you break through the surface and find yourself in a well-lit underground grotto. You paddle to the water's edge and notice a flight of stone steps. Raising yourself out of the water, you climb the stairs.

Soon you are at the top of the steps. It is brightly lit here. Before you is a panorama of monuments, sculptures, photographs, and paintings. You wander among these marvels and realize that you are seeing all of humanity's greatest artwork. Everything beautiful is here with no explanation of how it arrived. It is here simply for you to enjoy.

Once you have wandered to your satisfaction through the subterranean art museum, you realize you are slightly hungry. Thinking back, you recall the profusion of fruits back near the beach. You decide to return to the beach to satisfy your appetite and lie in the sun.

You plunge into the water of the grotto, and in a few leisurely strokes you swim back through the underwater opening to the moss-lined pool outside. Pulling yourself out of the water, you stride upstream to the waterfall and down the trail past the flowers and animals to the beach.

When you get near enough to the beach to hear the lapping of the waves, you see the abundant fruits and nuts. All around you are peaches, pears, apricots, bananas, apples, cherries, strawberries, mangoes, papayas, pomegranates, oranges, kiwis, pineapples, and every other edible fruit you have ever known.

Among these fruit trees are trees and plants bearing walnuts, almonds, filberts, Brazil nuts, coconuts, and peanuts. You eat as much as you want.

Once you have satisfied your appetite, you wander out to the beach and lie down on the warm sand. Bathed in the sun's radiance, you think about how calm, content, and powerful you feel. How often in recent months have you felt this good? Wouldn't your friends appreciate an experience like this?

You realize you are alone here, and as wonderful as it is, you have left your family, friends, and projects behind. This vacation was just what you needed, but there are relationships to affirm and expand, and tasks to push forward. The experience of your tropical paradise has given you the respite and reserve energy necessary to move ahead. You begin to look forward to your return.

Now that you know how to get to your tropical paradise, you know you can return without help in the future. This knowledge fuels your resolve to tackle your responsibilities with vigor.

You have a choice of boats to take home. One leaves in the afternoon, one in the early evening, and one after sunset. There will not be another boat to this isolated location for another month, and your responsibilities will not allow you to stay that long. You have to choose which of the three boats you would prefer to take and relax on the beach until its departure.

When the time comes to leave, you board the gangplank and stand at the rail while the boat chugs away. You gaze back at your island and remember all the day's experiences. They are yours to keep, to draw upon, and to add to whenever you choose to go back to your tropical paradise. But now you must return to the comfort of your own home.

Still feeling the relaxation of your paradise, breathe in deeply. On the third breath, slowly open your eyes.

Questions for reflection

Was this exercise pleasurable? How did it make you feel?

What aspects of your paradise pleased you the most? Which aspects were you indifferent about?

Did you feel any different once you had completed the exercise?

Did you feel any hesitation about leaving? Did you question whether you could find your way back again?

Why do you think this tropical paradise was so pleasant?

Why do you appreciate the beauty of the island but not the beauty of the world you see each day? Do you think it's possible to take from this experience an attitude that would enable you to appreciate your everyday world? How can you translate the beauty of a new environment to the beauty of a familiar environment that may be constantly changing?

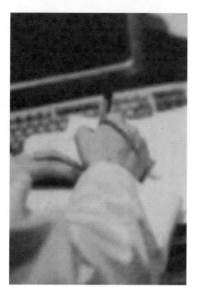

Work

Whether we love it or mostly endure it, work takes up the largest portion of our adult lives. Because work requires so much of our time and energy, it becomes a measure of our self-perception and place in the world. Sometimes, because it is a measure of our self-worth, we overexert ourselves and work too hard. We find that we can't accomplish our goals no matter how hard we strain; so we go on vacation to get away.

In this exercise, you can learn to "go on vacation" at work by approaching it from a positive, relaxed, well-centered state. You will see yourself in a stressful work situation and envision changes in your approach to it rather than trying to change the situation or the other people involved.

Preparation

To help you imagine a difficult situation at work, you might want to do this exercise at your workplace—early in the morning or late in the day when you are unlikely to be disturbed. If you are going to deal with a very tense situation in this image, however, you might prefer the relaxed surroundings of your home.

To succeed in this exercise, continually maintain a state of relaxation. If you become tense at any point, step back and relax again before continuing. Since this exercise partly involves imagining you are on vacation, you may want to practice the *Tropical Paradise* exercise to help you relax and visualize your vacation spot.

Now sit in a comfortable position, concentrate on your breathing, close your eyes, and begin step one.

Exercise

Step One—Take a vacation. For two or three minutes, create a setting in which you can feel warm, confident, and content. In this place, no demands are placed on you; all is peaceful and calm.

[*Pause*]

Step Two—Staying relaxed, without judgment or anger, take one minute as a disconnected observer to look at an actual event that has occurred at work. View yourself and others in a confrontation at the office. As you watch the event unfold, take note of any words, gestures, and behaviors that you wish to improve.

[*Pause*]

Step Three—Now go back on vacation for two minutes. You may return to your holiday spot or choose a different place to relax. Make sure you see, smell, feel, and hear the characteristic sensations there.

Step Four—Now reenter the situation at your workplace. This time you will see yourself at your best. Each word, gesture, and behavior is designed to move the situation forward to a satisfactory resolution, and you are in control. At this optimum level of performance, you maximize your skills and energy to their fullest.

Step Five—Once again, go on vacation, to the same or a different place. As you relax, notice whether you now feel a greater sense of strength or pride in yourself due to your most recent performance at the office. Once you feel completely relaxed, you will open your eyes and awaken to the office or home setting in which you began the exercise.

Questions for reflection

Were you able to relax on your initial vacation, knowing that you were about to deal with a problem at work?

Were you able to remain calm as you first ran through the confrontation at work? Did you find yourself having to stop, or rewind the scene?

In recalling the problem at work, did you catch yourself jumping to conclusions about what the other person or people did wrong? Did you have to fight a temptation to say, "If only he (or she) had done this"?

How did it feel to go on vacation a second time, after the first visit at work? Did you find it easy or hard to relax?

Was your second run-through at work a success? Were other people resistant? Were you surprised at how easy it was?

How did it feel to make "all the right moves"?

How did you feel during the final vacation?

Do you now feel ready to handle the next confrontation at work more successfully?

Little moments of stress can throw us in different ways. Depending on our character and the situation, we can either forget a mishap or let it wreck our whole day. Usually, we can laugh about it after enough time has passed, or if we see it happen to someone else.

This image allows you to observe someone else suffer a series of mishaps. It should provide some comic relief and help you prepare for mishaps that happen to you.

Mishaps

Preparation
Place yourself anywhere comfortable, shut your eyes, and relax.

Exercise
John Doe is about to wake up this morning to find everything go wrong. It will *not* be his best day.

John had planned to get up at seven, but a power outage near dawn stopped his electric alarm clock. When John wakes up and realizes by the sunlight that it's later than seven, he leaps out of bed and sends a valuable lamp crashing to the floor.

Having no time to clean up the fragments, John stumbles into the bathroom and steps into the shower. A blast of ice-cold water hits his bare skin. The power failure strikes again! John is definitely awake now.

The chilling shower over, he steps up to the sink to shave. He nonchalantly grabs a can of shaving cream, and as soon as he slaps some on his face his skin begins to sting. Taking a good look at the can, John finds he has applied hair remover to his sensitive chin, cheeks, and upper lip. Although he frantically washes his face, the lower half has already become red and splotchy.

John gets dressed. While yanking on his shoes, he breaks a shoestring. With no spare laces in sight, he pulls on a pair of old, beat-up running shoes. "Can't hurt to wear them at the office for just one day," he tells himself.

John, now dressed, leaves the house and gets into his car. No sooner has he buckled up, than he realizes that his briefcase is still in the house. He runs back and forgets his keys, which are now locked in the car. He can't get into the house and he can't get into the car.

Fortunately, he has his wallet on him, so he catches a cab to work. Miraculously, he arrives only thirty minutes late.

When John gets to his office, he learns that his secretary has quit. At least the four business letters that have to go out today are done. He gets a cup of coffee, sits down to look over the letters, and signs them.

The phone rings and his buddy Jerry tells him he's fixed him up with a blind date, "a real gorgeous blonde," for tonight. "She's smart," says Jerry. "You'll like her."

With the way things have gone so far, John has his doubts. But it is hard to meet people these days, so he thanks Jerry and accepts his offer. Jerry's call reminds him that he needs to call the locksmith so he can get back into his home tonight.

John makes the call and returns to the letters on his desk—which are lying in a dark brown puddle. Apparently the Styrofoam cup has leaked its contents all over John's desk. The letters will have to be retyped, and since the secretary quit, John will have to do it.

John doesn't type very well, but he has to get these letters out. He starts to type and suddenly the typewriter buzzes loudly and stops dead.

John's boss comes in with the morning mail. There's a magazine in the pile, and John is sure it's his first issue of the *New Yorker,* which he had ordered when a school kid came to the door selling subscriptions.

The magazine turns out to be *Monthly Witchcraft.* Confused, John flips through several pages of spells and tries to figure out what happened. *Did I check the wrong box on the form,* he wonders.

When he looks up, his boss smirks and nods toward the magazine. "Think some of those would help you and your department?" his boss asks.

Embarrassed, John mumbles something about some documents that need to be photocopied and makes a hasty retreat to the copy machine.

Thankful for having avoided an awkward conversation, John puts down the first page and presses the print button. A red light flashes on the copier; the machine is out of toner.

John fetches replacement toner and opens a panel on the copier. He tries to unscrew the cap on the toner tank, but it seems to be stuck. Trying to wrench it off, he loses his grip on the replacement bottle and it splashes down the front of his suit, staining it with black ink. Staring gloomily at his blackened suit, John wonders, *Is there any way to make a copy of myself to tackle the rest of the day?*

John decides to leave early for lunch and put the morning's mishaps behind him. After the server takes his order for cream of celery soup, he looks dejectedly at his ink-stained shirtfront and slacks. *How am I going to get through my afternoon meeting with the company executives when I'm such a mess,* he wonders.

Just then, John's server, carrying his bowl of soup, collides into a busboy and spills the soup all over him, providing a creamy topping for the ink on his clothes. "At least the soup isn't hot," he tells himself wearily as he makes his way to the washroom. "Thank heaven my vacation starts next week."

The afternoon is an endless series of business meetings. John's strategy is to sit at the far end of the table from the bigwigs and say as little as possible. All he wants is to get through the rest of the day unnoticed and go home.

The final meeting of the day involves the top executives in the company and several powerful clients. John has played a large role in arranging this deal. Fortunately, he doesn't have to make the presentation, so he merely nods from his seat whenever his name is mentioned.

Suddenly the door of the boardroom bursts open. A

shapely female with dark hair and long eyelashes steps in wearing nothing but a see-through negligee over bra and panties. She slinks over to John and begins to sing "Happy Birthday" while removing her scanty garments. Some of the men sit in stunned silence, others guffaw and applaud.

Who sent me a strip-o-gram, John wonders. *It's not my birthday! My birthday was six months ago.* It is not until the stripper has removed nearly everything and is wrapping her lingerie around John's neck that an office clerk runs in and announces the birthday message was meant for John Smith on the next floor.

The meeting has broken up, and John Doe's workday is finally over. After taking a taxi home, he looks for the locksmith who was supposed to let him into his house. There's no sign of him. Dejected, John leans wearily against the locked front door—and it swings open!

One look at the total mess inside is enough to tell John that his house has been robbed. Tables and chairs are overturned, drawers pulled out, and shelves swept clean. His television and stereo are gone, and the closets have been cleared of all his good clothes. Stunned, John keeps telling himself that a window must have been open and a hurricane did this.

John calls and reports the theft to the police. Then he briefly considers canceling the blind date, but he doesn't know how to contact the woman. He manages to throw together a makeshift outfit and heads for the bar.

By this time John is absolutely sure that nothing good can happen to him now, so he orders a huge Bloody Mary. At the moment the bartender hands him the big red glass, a gorgeous woman in a black dress walks up to him. "Are you John Doe?" she asks. "I'm Laura, your date."

Stunned by his good fortune, John nods and takes a gulp of his drink. Instead of a cool mouthful, however, he gets a scorching sensation on his tongue. The bartender accidentally poured in a big dollop of Tabasco sauce! The pain is searing, and John involuntarily coughs the horrid mixture down the front of Laura's dress. "I don't believe this," he groans to himself.

Laura takes it with a sense of humor, though, and after a quick visit to the washroom she is back as if nothing has happened. After forty minutes of drinks and pleasant conversation, John has just about put all the bad experiences of the day behind him.

After a while, Laura says she'd like to see John's place. He tries to explain that it's a mess, but Laura insists it doesn't matter. So John reaches for his wallet—to find it has also been stolen. Laura has to pay for all their drinks, but she doesn't mind.

When the taxi drops them off at John's place, the police are there. All of John's stolen belongings except for his clothes have been located and returned.

Since the power is still out, the officers provide some candles. Laura sits patiently on the sofa while John fills out ownership and property forms to reclaim what's been found and adequately describe what's still missing. He also reports his stolen wallet. During this lengthy process, the power returns.

Once the formalities are concluded and the officers

leave, John can finally pay attention to his date. To mellow out, he plugs in his antique stereo, puts on his favorite LP, and goes to the kitchen to find something to serve Laura.

When he enters the kitchen, he sees water all over the floor. Because the electricity has been off all day, the refrigerator has defrosted, and the food is spoiled or at least suspect. There's nothing to serve John's guest.

At that moment, tinny music with chipmunk voices comes in from the living room. John's stereo is playing at 78 rpm's. The burglars must have broken it in their haste. Although he's out of money, John tries to suggest the two of them go out for a bite, but Laura's had enough. Gently but firmly, she says good night.

By now, John's too tired to do much more than look at the mail. He learns he's been chosen as a contestant for the Price is Right the following week. *That's great,* he thinks; *it'll fit right in with my vacation.* The second envelope reveals that he's been collared for jury duty the same week.

John collapses on the bed. As he drifts into sleep, he relaxes with the knowledge that tomorrow has to be a better day.

Questions for reflection

Did you find this exercise amusing? What events did you find most funny? Why?

Mishaps

Had any of these incidents ever happened to you? How did you deal with them at the time?

Was it all funny to you, or did tension build at some point? Were there any events that provoked anxiety in you?

After a certain amount of time passes, does your attitude about such mishaps change? Do you tell other people about what happened to amuse them? How long does it take you to leave your tension or pain behind and laugh at yourself?

Can you think of a mishap that upset you when it happened to you but made you laugh when it happened to someone else? Why was there a difference?

The passage of time seems to relax our tensions so that we can laugh at incidents that upset us when they occurred. How might you learn to relax, perhaps even laugh, the instant a mishap occurs in your life?

Inner-directed images

The images in this section relate to the core values and experiences—your self-esteem, needs, desires, fears, and apprehensions—that make you unique and shape your thoughts and actions. They focus on characteristics and qualities that originate from deep within. Use them to expand your awareness of your inner self so you may better understand how you think and feel as well as the reasons behind those thoughts and feelings.

Imagine yourself as . . .   p. 78

In this exercise, you will imagine yourself as various objects and creatures in five different categories. You should make quick choices and rely on your instincts to arrive at them.

Pine forest   p. 80

Experiences with nature often put us in touch with feelings of serenity, stability, and strength. This exercise will help you explore some of those feelings within yourself.

Rejuvenating walk   p. 84

As we travel through different stages in our lives, various circumstances and people affect us. Sometimes looking at the past from our present perspective enables us to see objectively where we have been and who we have become. In this exercise, you will revisit and reexperience your past to develop a new awareness of yourself.

Decision dive   p. 88

This exercise helps you check your decision-making ability. As you go through the image, be aware of any feelings or body sensations you may experience— especially when you have to make the decision to dive.

In this exercise, you will imagine yourself as various objects and creatures in five different categories. You should make quick choices and rely upon your instincts to arrive at them.

Note: You might choose to do this exercise with someone else and ask, "If you imagined me as (something from the exercise) what would I be?" Once you have each shared your perceptions, discuss why you made those choices.

Imagine yourself as . . .

Preparation

Choose any comfortable, quiet setting. While seated, take three deep breaths. On the last exhale, close your eyes.

Exercise

Imagine yourself as the following:

A house—select a size and color. Then choose a style: ranch, Victorian, Early American, modern, or something else.

A body of water—a small glass of water, a brook, a river, a lake, or an ocean. Now examine this body of water and see what is in or around it. Notice if it is moving, and if so, how fast or slow.

An automobile—choose a type, model and color.

A piece of athletic equipment—a soccer ball, football, hockey puck, skates, bat, ball, glove, net, barbell, piece of clothing, canoe, or anything else.

A four-legged animal—what kind, what characteristics?

Questions for reflection

Examine the choices you made from the categories. What aspects of your personality do you suppose each image represents?

Is there anything that the images you chose have in common?

Did any of your choices surprise you?

Did any of your choices puzzle you?

Experiences with nature often put us in touch with feelings of serenity, stability, and strength. This exercise will help you explore some of those feelings within yourself.

Preparation

Breathe deeply and relax with each exhalation. As your body relaxes, allow your eyes to close, continue breathing deeply, and begin this exercise.

Pine forest

Exercise

Breathe deeply in and out. As you breathe in, you will begin to smell the aroma of pine. Faint at first, the pungent, fresh smell of pine gradually grows stronger and stronger. The pleasant pine smell now drifts up through your nostrils with each inhalation. The smell is very strong now and beckons you to enter an immense pine forest.

Once in the forest, you can see the tall dark green pine trees gathered serenely about you. The forest is pitch black in some places; in others, you notice bright shafts of golden sunlight shooting between the branches, lighting up clusters of needles and gnarled bark.

The pine smell fills the air around you. As you walk among the trees, you hear the soft crackle of dry needles underfoot. A soft, full silence seems to press into your ears and fills your mind with calm. Only an occasional bird cry breaks the marvelous quiet.

As you look about the forest, you notice one pine tree that attracts you. As your attraction grows, begin to move closer to the tree. Allow yourself to move as close as you like and gaze at the trunk before you. Notice the color and the pattern of the bark—where it looks smooth and where it looks rough. Observe the thickness of the trunk where it meets the earth. It is solid and powerful.

Now visually trace the line of the trunk upward, to where the sturdy branches reach out into space. Thickest where they meet the trunk, they grow thin as they reach firmly yet gracefully outward. Notice the pinecones with their gradually narrowing layers of brittle petals. Thin, finely pointed needles festoon the branches.

Reach out and touch the needles. Feel them against your skin. If you wish, explore the ridges of a pinecone with your finger and touch the bark of a branch, feeling its texture against your skin. You may feel a few drops of sap as you touch the branch.

When you have finished exploring the exterior of your tree, imagine what it would be like to become the tree, to share its shape, textures, and sensations, and live its life. Begin to merge with the tree. Notice your sensations and feelings as you do.

Are you comfortable? You may change your tree in any way you wish to make it more comfortable to you: increase or decrease your height; extend or retract your branches; invite other trees to move closer to you, or cause the nearest trees to move away. Make whatever adjustments you desire to feel entirely comfortable as a pine tree.

Beginning with your outer covering, explore your needles and pinecones. Next, focus on your bark, and note how it feels to have this thick layer of rough skin surround and protect you. Become aware of your branches, from the thickest at the bottom to the thinnest at the top. Feel their firm, wooden appendages reaching out from your trunk. Notice the contrast in temperature between your branches at the top, warmed by the sun, and your lower branches covered in shade.

Next, focus your attention on your trunk. Feel the circulatory system moving water inside you and out to your branches. Feel nourished by the water coursing through you. Feel how solidly and sturdily you support your branches.

Next, become aware of your roots below the ground. Notice the way your trunk branches out underground into a network of roots. Feel how deeply and firmly these roots reach into the earth. Become aware of how sure and stable a grounding they provide, and how they hold you firmly in place.

Now become aware of the roots of nearby pines and of the extensive underground network of intertwining roots between rocks and earth. Follow some of these roots upward, above ground, noticing how you feel as you become aware of these other pine trees.

When you are through exploring, focus once again on your pine tree, but retain a sense of your neighbors' existence, below and above ground. Notice the feelings and sensations of your needles, branches, trunk, and roots, and those of neighboring trees.

Now once again, focus on your pine tree's circulatory system and its exchange of air with the atmosphere. The tree "inhales" carbon dioxide and "exhales" oxygen.

Begin to notice your breathing, and the pulsing of your heart and circulatory system. Feel and hear yourself breathing deeply, and in a moment, open your eyes and return to the place in which you started this exercise.

Questions for reflection

How did you feel when you found yourself in the pine forest?

How did you feel when you identified with your pine tree? Did you change your tree or its surroundings in any way?

As you explored the inner life of your tree, did any feelings or sensations surprise or please you?

Were you aware of the other trees? Of the forest? Did you have any feelings about them?

When the exercise was over, did you experience any feelings of inner strength or oneness with nature?

As we travel through different stages in our lives, various circumstances and people affect us. Sometimes looking at our past from our present perspective enables us to see objectively where we have been and who we have become. In this exercise, you will revisit and reexperience your past to develop a new awareness of yourself.

Preparation

If you are at home, you may wish to relax in a comfortable room that promotes fond memories. Prepare to remember your past in this relaxed setting and close your eyes.

Rejuvenating walk

Exercise

Imagine that you are strolling down one of your hometown streets, a street you've walked along so many times that you no longer notice what's there.

It is the present, and on this particular day you are feeling somewhat adventurous as you pass familiar stores. At this particular moment, you glance sideways into a store window and notice an object you lost when you were much younger. As you look at the object, recall various experiences associated with it and the feelings caused by its disappearance.

Now notice your reflection in the glass. Become aware of your reflection and begin to see it as a shorter version of yourself. The window reflects the image of the you

84

who had lost the object. Spend some time examining this different yet recognizable person and slowly begin to identify with that image. Allow the person in the reflection and you to become one and the same.

Now start heading down the street again. Everything looks bigger than it did before. The cars driving by look larger, and they seem to move faster. The store signs are higher, and you have to crane your neck to see them.

A dog comes running toward you. It is a big dog, perhaps a dog you remember while growing up in your home town. You look each other over, someone calls the dog, and it turns and runs away.

You continue your walk. When you reach the corner, look down and notice that the curb is much closer to you than before. During the walk from the store window to the curb, you have shrunk even further in size and years.

You see no stoplight or signal. You will have to run across the street through the heavy traffic. There is hardly a break between the cars. You see your chance approaching, get ready, now run.

Running with your eyes focused on the distant curb, you hear a horn blast, very near and very loud, but you make it to the far curb and stop to catch your breath. Feel your chest press out against your clothing and the blood pound in your temples. You rest for a minute.

After a short while, you look around and notice that you are in your neighborhood. A person you knew from long ago appears. You recognize each other and talk for a few moments.

Rejuvenating walk

Soon you say good-bye and continue your walk. Eventually you find the place where you grew up. You make your way to the entrance. The doorknob may be hard to reach or turn for someone your size and age, but you manage to go indoors.

You are now inside the house, and you slowly look around. Allow yourself to examine each object you see as thoroughly as you wish. If there is a characteristic smell to this room, take note of it.

One of the items you find is an object you associate closely with the parent or guardian who took care of you. You walk over and examine it carefully. The object makes you feel both the person's presence and your own emotions.

Continuing to look about the house, you notice a sign of achievement that was put on display. You had done something that made everyone proud of you and this object commemorates that happy event. Looking at it, you can relive the achievement.

You wander about the house until you come upon something that belonged to you, and only you. Perhaps it came into your possession through some happy circumstance. Perhaps it is dear to you because of all the experiences associated with it. You allow yourself to recall those good times.

Soon it is time to leave. You walk out the door and find yourself moving into a later time, into a time after you had left home. Feel yourself grow physically into the person of that time; you become bigger and stronger. This process brings you right up to the present moment as you return from a walk into your youth and come back with those memories intact, finding yourself once again in the place from which you started. Relax and open your eyes.

Questions for reflection

What was the object in the window that you had lost?

Did you recognize the fear of dashing across a busy street as a young person?

Who was the person you met on the street? What did you say to each other?

How did you feel when you saw your old home? How did it feel to be inside it again?

What sort of feeling did the object associated with your parent or guardian elicit in you?

What achievement of yours was commemorated? How did you feel when you saw the object that commemorated it?

What experiences and feelings were connected to the special article that was yours alone?

Did you notice anything that was unfamiliar about the interior of your old home or the objects inside it?

How did it feel to grow up out of the past? Were you relieved, regretful, or pleased?

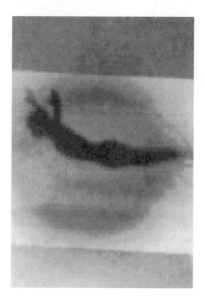

Decision dive

In this exercise, you can check your decision-making ability. As you go through the image, be aware of any feelings or body sensations you may experience—especially when you have to make the decision to dive.

Preparation
Sit comfortably in a firm chair, placed facing the sun or a low-watt bulb. Close your eyes and focus on feeling the heat of the sun (or imagine the bulb as the sun). Allow yourself to feel the warmth of the sun on your face and neck, and over your upper body, steadily caressing your skin. As you feel the warmth spreading over your entire body, you see the dim yellow glow of a small sun. The glow gets brighter and brighter, and you find yourself at the edge of a sunny wheat field.

Exercise
Standing alone, you see the midday sun brightly shining on the sun-drenched field stretching into the distance, blending into the horizon. As you stand in the blistering sun, you feel uncomfortably hot. Your skin feels warm, and beads of perspiration form and trickle down your face. As you reach up to wipe them off, you breathe the hot and heavy air.

The heat continues to rise. Your mouth and throat are dry and your body heavy. You feel thirsty and decide to look for water. Since you see only the wide expanse of wheat in the hot sun before you, you decide to explore other directions. You look to your right and see a dark green forest about one hundred yards away. Moving forward, you notice your damp clothes clinging to your body.

Very soon, you approach the edge of a forest, and you step into the cool shade. Beneath the green canopy of leaves, the air is cool and refreshing. Take in any sounds or smells, and touch anything that interests you.

In the distance you hear the sound of water. Faint at first, the sound grows louder as you move towards it. The trees begin to thin out, and you see sunlight ahead. You approach a clearing and explore it, noticing that it stops at the edge of a canyon. To the right and left, the canyon stretches into the distance. A twenty-foot gap lies between your side of the canyon and the other. Not far away, you observe a rickety footbridge made of rope and wooden planks that crosses the canyon.

As you approach the bridge, take a moment to look into the canyon. The bottom drops about sixty feet and is completely dry and littered with jagged rocks. You realize the only way to cross the canyon is to walk across the footbridge.

You can still hear the water beyond the canyon, and you begin to feel hot again in the direct sunlight. As you step onto the first plank, the bridge sways under your weight and you hear the ropes creak. Moving forward, you hear behind you the sound of planks striking the rocks below. You realize that the bridge is disintegrating and that you must keep moving forward.

Decision dive

As you plant your foot on the other side, you hear the ropes snap. You look back and see the last planks clatter down to the floor of the canyon. You turn to survey the terrain before you. The land has become increasingly rocky. As you walk, you can hear the sound of water getting dramatically louder. You know that you are near the source. Your body feels scorched, and your muscles ache. Your throat is parched, and you are thirsty.

The horizon forms a distinct line and you realize that you are approaching a cliff. Coming from somewhere below the cliff you hear the very loud sound of water, and you move forward to investigate. When you reach the edge, you look down and see a steep seventy-foot drop into a wide expanse of water.

When you look up, you see that you are standing on a barren, flat plateau stretching out for miles in all directions. Behind you is a deep drop into a canyon filled with rocks. On either side of you is a rocky plateau. In front of you is a seventy-foot drop into water. You must decide to dive or remain stranded at the top of the cliff.

Some distance away, you can see the peaks of several large rocks. But in the water below, you cannot see the bottom or any rocks. The water looks deep enough for a safe dive.

The sun is beating down on you, and each moment you wait, you get hotter and more tired. Be aware of all your feelings, thoughts, and sensations as you arrive at a decision. Keep in mind that you are capable of making the dive safely, and that your discomfort and danger increase each moment you postpone the decision. You must decide to dive or not.

[*Pause*]

Note: If you decide not to dive, imagine being in the water and skip the next paragraph.

Walk to the edge of the cliff and put your body into position. Take a deep breath and prepare to dive. Now push off and dive toward the water. Notice your feelings and sensations while you dive. As you move through the air, you will begin to feel confident. You feel increasingly exhilarated by the weightless feeling of your body moving through space. Soon, you penetrate the surface of the water. It feels shockingly cold, but delightfully refreshing. You rise to the surface and begin to swim around, enjoying the feel of rushing water against your body.

Not far away is a sandy beach, and you swim toward it. As you reach shallow water, you stand up and walk onto the beach. Feeling refreshed but tired, you lie down to rest and dry off. As you lie there, you can feel the sun warming and drying your skin and relaxing your muscles. You feel sleepy, and close your eyes. Soon, you sense a yellow glow through your eyelids. You see it faintly at first, but gradually notice the glow brighten. As it gets brighter, you open your eyes and return to the present.

Questions for reflection

How did you feel when you found yourself in the wheat field?

Decision dive

How did you feel when you began to explore the forest?
When you heard the water?

How did you feel when you moved into the clearing
and saw the canyon and footbridge? How did you feel
just before, during, and after you crossed the bridge?
When you saw it collapse?

How did you feel as you moved across the plateau?
When you discovered it ended in a cliff over water?
How did you feel as you realized you had to make the
decision?

What were your thoughts, feelings, and sensations
before, during, and after you made your decision? Did
any options other than making the dive occur to you? If
you rejected them, why? What made you finally choose
one option? Did any of your responses surprise you?

What made you most want to dive? Your thirst, your
discomfort in the heat, or something else?

How did you feel as you dove?

Did any of your responses to the situations in the
exercise remind you of your responses to situations in
your life? Did anything feel new to you?

What did you learn about yourself through this
exercise?

Periods of transition, development, and growth are sometimes difficult, whether approached with apprehension or with enthusiasm and high expectations. This exercise emphasizes the inherent loveliness in human transformation by having you imagine changing from a caterpillar into a butterfly.

Preparation

Sit in any comfortable setting that evokes a garden environment. An actual garden in which you can observe a caterpillar at work would be an ideal setting for this exercise. As you concentrate on this scene, close your eyes.

Caterpillar to butterfly

Exercise

Today you find yourself in a garden of flowers, vegetables, and herbs. As you look around, you spot a caterpillar making its way through this foliage. Observe its progress intently and see how its body moves, where it hesitates, and when it presses on.

As you observe the progress of the caterpillar, imagine that you become it: a slow, awkward, funny creature. Now, as a caterpillar, you develop a rhythm to your movement that requires effort from your entire body. Movement is a major accomplishment, requiring maneuvers around so many obstacles that you wonder why you have to keep on moving without pausing.

You work your way up the stem of a leafy bush.
Pausing at a shiny green leaf, you decide to chew on it.
Even dining is a whole body affair. You must anchor
most of your legs on the leaf and slowly bend the top
half of your body over while you eat the leaf.

Having eaten your fill, you return to the main stem to
climb some more. You are searching for a high but
secure place to fasten yourself, for something inside you
tells you that it is now time to rest and prepare for a
momentous change.

Now you are about to begin the transformation. As the
caterpillar, choose a secure place to anchor. Begin to
produce delicate silky threads that stick to your feet,
then slowly begin to envelope you. They wind around
your whole body, like a warm flannel sheet, and finally
cover your head in a chrysalis of silk.

Now you are encased in the cocoon. The endless
inching across flowers, leaves, and sidewalks has
ended. You have plenty of time to go over your
thoughts and feelings. How does it feel to be encased in
the cocoon? Is it hot? Is it hard to breathe? Is it soft and
cozy? Is it cool?

While you are inside, strange and wonderful things are
happening to you. It is too dark to see anything, but
you can feel your skin, your very structure shift and
reassemble. It is as if all the molecules of your body
have unfastened to migrate and form new attachments.
Although you are cuddled up in the cocoon, there is
astounding activity going on here.

At the same time, you know that life outside is oblivi-
ous to what you are becoming. The last anyone may

have noticed, they saw an ungainly caterpillar stop for a rest. You allow your excitement to grow as you anticipate the moment of release when everyone will see what has happened to you.

The time has come! You tense your muscles and push out, feeling and hearing the soft rip of the cocoon. You are very conscious of the work and the emotions involved in getting free of the cocoon.

You are now free. You rest on the branch for a while and glance at your transformed body still moist from the cocoon. You savor this instant of triumph after all the preparation, the transformation, and the struggle to break out. The sun's heat cleanses and dries you—it shines over and through you as you feel your wings fill with a potent life force.

Now take some time to carefully scrutinize your new size and color. With your present body, you could hide a number of caterpillars—those earnest, hardworking versions of your former self. Soon you will take wing and survey the expanse of the garden.

Once in the air, you can view the whole of your former world at a glance. Below you are the flowers, vegetables, and herbs where you once toiled. How small it all seems today! With one last glance, you turn to fly off to new lands and achievements.

Keeping that overwhelming feeling of accomplishment, become aware of your own setting in this garden environment. Relax with each cleansing breath. Now it is time to open your eyes and awaken.

Questions for reflection

How did it feel to move as a caterpillar? Did that feeling remind you of any times in your life as a human when you felt ungainly and unattractive or sluggish?

Did you feel anything positive in the rhythm of crawling as a caterpillar?

What were your feelings when you were encased in the cocoon? What did you think about?

Could you feel your body changing in the cocoon? Did you feel that you were making it happen or that it was happening to you?

Did you imagine what was going on outside the cocoon?

How did it feel to push out of the chrysalis?

What kind of butterfly did you become? What size, shape, and color?

What did the garden look like when you took flight?

Did you plan on flying anywhere?

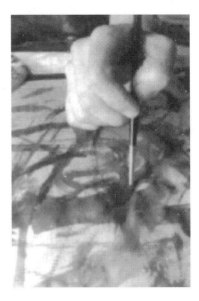

W e often catch ourselves dreaming of all the hobbies we'd pursue if only we had the time and money. Perhaps we desire to do photography, boat or house construction, sketching, painting, or sculpting. Sometimes we get around to it; often we don't.

In this exercise you will have the opportunity to explore the creativity that resides in you. By mentally creating a work of art—with unlimited time and all the materials you'll need—you incur no risk, no tension, and no judgment. You can adjust anything you like at any time, or even destroy the work and start over, with a minimum of fuss.

Art

Preparation
Relax in a quiet room. Close your eyes and take three deep breaths. On the third breath you will find yourself more relaxed. Allow your breath to carry you into a studio or other place where you feel you may express your creative artistic energies. Take whatever time you need to establish a place that has the best lighting, space, furnishings, and equipment for your work. Once you have the ideal location, you are ready to begin.

Exercise
Now that you have a work space, you can begin your art piece. It may be any size, shape, and color you wish. You can work with oils, acrylics, watercolors, wood, steel, clay, glass, ink, pencil, neon, water, trash, plant life, plastic, string, paper, canvas, or any combination

thereof. The final product might have practical applications but it certainly doesn't have to. As you construct it, feel free to add to it, subtract from it, change it in any manner you wish until it is just the way you want.

Perhaps you don't have a particular end result in mind. Allow yourself to experiment for a while without having to worry about what you make. Throw things together; toss them around; try anything that comes into your head. Something wonderful may happen, but if it doesn't, you can dispose of it and try something else. You have unlimited time and materials, after all.

You don't have to finish your masterpiece in one session. You don't even have to feel you've made a good start on whatever will be the final art work. If you have to leave, or *want* to leave, everything will be here in your studio whenever you come back. When you are ready to leave your studio, concentrate on your art work, relax, and take three deep breaths. With your third breath, exhale and open your eyes, returning to your quiet surroundings.

Question for reflection
If your work is INCOMPLETE:

Do you have a sense of what you were trying to achieve? If not, what materials did you prefer experimenting with? What colors and shapes attracted you the most.

Would you rather experiment or finish a piece?

Do you find yourself comfortable with making a mess and using up a lot of supplies to experiment, or are you a more careful and methodical artist?

Is there anyone you feel would like to see what you are working on? Is there anyone who might be able to help you realize what you're after? Is there anyone for whom you are specifically trying to design this piece?

If your work is COMPLETED:

How long did it take you to identify what you wanted to create? Did you know what you wanted from the first or arrive at it by trying different things?

Did the execution go smoothly or did you make a lot of changes on the way?

What do you think the materials, size, and colors of this art piece might suggest about its creator?

Did you ever feel like trashing your work along the way and starting over?

Can you think of anyone you would like to show this masterpiece to?

Now that you have designed your art piece and executed it mentally, how difficult would it be to really bring it into the world? Would you like to? Are there any other ideas you'd like to try?

Note: Once you have designed a piece of art completely in your head, it will be that much easier to bring it to life when you take the time and effort.

Guilt

Guilt is the most unnecessary of emotions. We impose it on ourselves, and the longer we hold onto it, the more complicated and tenacious it becomes. The inertia of doing nothing makes it worse.

When we speak of guilt we often say we are being "eaten away inside," or "carrying the weight of the world on our shoulders." The mere repetition of the words "I am guilty" and "I feel guilty" seems to physically weigh us down. But when freed from guilt, we may actually feel uplifted physically.

In this exercise, you will practice letting go of the burden of guilt by imagining it as a bag full of rocks that you end up throwing away.

Preparation

First, relax. Imagine a safe, quiet place and feel its calming influence. Once you are fully relaxed, imagine you are returning from a vacation to face the world and pick up all your old psychic baggage. This baggage consists primarily of things that make you feel guilty; things you tell yourself you should do or should not have done—issues at work or school, with friends, or family; financial issues; or anything else. You are going to change these concerns into a load of rocks that you will carry in a sack.

Exercise

You are walking down a road with a bag of rocks slung over your shoulder. Each of these rocks represents an issue, an action, a feeling, or a memory that gives you a guilty feeling. The bag is unbearably heavy, and though most of the time you do not think about it, it is still a lot of work to carry this load. Your hands are sore from gripping the bag, and the neck of it digs into your shoulder, which throbs and aches.

Someone you choose approaches you on the road. You are going to talk to this person about the stones in your sack. If much of your guilt revolves around a particular person, you might choose to meet him or her; or you may meet a friendly stranger instead.

You are about to share what is in the sack, exposing yourself without fear, because the other person is ready to listen and wants to understand. As you talk, you will remove rocks from the bag one by one and put them aside, thereby lessening the weight you will have to carry when it is time to start down the road again.

The two of you sit down to talk. Remove the first large stone from the bag and show it to your listener. While the two of you stare at this weight you have had to carry around, describe the issue it represents. Tell the other person the situation and chain of events that brought about this guilty concern. If there was an actual event, describe that next. Finally, explain your perceptions and feelings about what you did or failed to do.

The rock is a comforting diversion. The two of you can contemplate it instead of staring uncomfortably at each other. As you talk about your guilt, you realize you won't have to carry this stone anymore.

The other person has little to say, but you can tell from their facial expressions that you are understood. You are unburdening yourself of weight you had been carrying alone. Your listener is understanding and accepting.

Once you have fully explained the issue represented by the first rock, toss it as far away from you as you can. Reach into the sack and remove a second rock. Take as much time as you need to remove all the rocks and discuss the issues they represent. Be sure to cover the history, the actual incident if there is one, and your perceptions and feelings about the guilty concern. As you finish with each stone, push or throw it out of your sight.

[*Pause*]

The sack is empty now. All the stones have been disposed of. You have talked out all your feelings of guilt, and your patient listener smiles. That's all there is to it! Now you can get up and continue walking in whatever direction you wish to go. Hold onto the empty sack as a reminder of what was once in it. Notice how easy it is to stride along with all of your weight gone. Your thoughts are lighter, your senses clearer, and all the muscles that ached and strained feel fine now. The way is clear.

Questions for reflection

How large a sack did you imagine you carried? Do you think of yourself as more or less guilt-ridden than the average person?

Whom did you meet on the road? Why do you feel it was appropriate to talk to this person about your guilty concerns?

Is there anyone else you might have spoken to but were afraid to?

Did you find it difficult to talk about guilt?

Looking at all the concerns you raised, do you think they mainly involve guilt over things you did or things you failed to do?

Did you feel any pleasure or relief about discussing these worries and tossing the stones aside?

How do you feel now that you have emptied the bag? Did you share everything you wanted to?

Your oracle

When we are children, adults seem to be fountains of wisdom. They tell us what words mean, how to do our homework, and how to handle situations with other people. As we grow up, however, we learn that adults are fallible. We turn to specialists for a broadened perspective and to friends for advice. Yet none of them are entirely dependable; they are not like the Oracle of Delphi through which the gods spoke to humans. In the end, the only real source of wisdom lies within yourself. You are your own oracle.

During this exercise, you may consult your oracle for advice on concerns of your choosing. Consider your encounter with your oracle as a consultation, and try to maintain an open and receptive attitude toward everything you hear. By doing this, you will absorb more of the experience, and will have more to work with later on.

Preparation
Before beginning the exercise, screw a low-watt light bulb into a shadeless lamp. Get in a comfortable position and sit close enough to the lamp to stare at the lighted bulb.

Exercise
Stare at the lighted bulb in front of you. The outline of the bulb may begin to blur, and you may see a glowing spot of light surrounded by a hazy aura. Eventually, the spot of light may begin to shimmer. Your eyelids will

become heavy and your body will relax. Allow your eyelids to close, and feel your body relax. Even with your eyes closed, you can see a shimmering light that beckons you. Follow this light as it leads you to the base of a hill on a beautiful, starlit night.

As you look up, you see the clear midnight-blue sky, studded with thousands of brightly glowing stars. By the light of the stars, you see that the hill before you is bare, except for some rocks lining a narrow path leading toward the top. You also see more low, quiet hills in all directions around you.

Now, as you begin to climb, you can hear the sounds of rocks underfoot. As you continue climbing, you look toward the top of the hill. Soon, you see some white pillars rising over the crest. As the pillars loom larger and larger, you see the form of a white temple, glistening in the starlight.

As you move toward the temple, you see three steps leading up to a pair of heavy wooden doors. You open the doors and enter the dimly lit interior of the temple, pausing for a moment to allow your eyes to adjust to the dim light. You are in a large rectangular room with marble floors and walls. In the middle of the room is a well, made of stones. As you reach the well, you peer over the edge. Gazing down, you begin to make out clear water at the bottom of the deep well, which makes you feel thirsty and tired.

When you look up, you see a bucket on a rope attached to the side of the well. You take the bucket and lower it until you hear the splash as it hits the water. Then you haul up the bucket and sip some of the cool water. You drink until you are no longer thirsty. Then you sprinkle some water on your forehead. As the drops touch your forehead, you feel tingly and energized.

You replace the bucket by the side of the well and see a dense white mist rise from the well and move into the room. The mist dissolves and you see the shape of a living being, your oracle, now standing before you. Breathe deeply, feeling completely relaxed. As you observe your oracle, notice your thoughts and feelings. Remember that you intend to listen to whatever the oracle says and to observe the oracle's actions.

Your oracle communicates to you that you both have a limited amount of time together, but during that time, you can ask whatever questions you want. Think carefully about what advice you need, and then pose your questions to your oracle. After you ask your questions, see how your oracle responds. You may ask your questions now.

[*Pause*]

After some time has passed, your oracle tells you it is now time to go, but you may return for a consultation whenever you wish. All you need to do is walk up the hill, enter the temple, sip water from the well, and your oracle will emerge.

You express your thanks and leave the temple, walking back out through the open doors. As you leave and walk down the steps, you can hear the doors close behind you. While walking toward the bottom of the hill, you again hear the stones crunching underfoot. Upon reaching the bottom of the hill, you direct your gaze upward. Soon your eyes find a particularly bright star, brighter than all the others.

As you gaze at the star, it may begin to shimmer. Soon, your eyelids begin to feel heavy and they close. Through your closed eyelids you still see a hazy shimmering light. When you are ready to return to your room, open your eyes, feeling awake and alert.

Questions for reflection

Did your oracle take any particular form?

Did you have any feelings when your oracle appeared?

Did any of the questions you chose to ask surprise you? Did any of the questions you chose not to ask surprise you?

If your oracle answered, did its words spark any insights? Did they puzzle or surprise you? If your oracle did not answer, how did you feel?

When it was time to say good-bye to your oracle, how did you feel?

How did you feel when your oracle invited you to return?

Are there questions you wish you had asked your oracle, or would want to ask in a future consultation?

Stepping out of time

People spend much of their energy fighting to control time. They find themselves stretching it, stealing it, or feeling they never have enough of it. All of us could learn to use our time better. In this fantasy, you will remove all constraints to clarify your current use of time and discover ways to improve the ways you use it.

Note: This exercise creates situations that you must imagine on your own; you will not be guided through them.

Preparation
This exercise can be used anywhere at any time. Select a place that is as quiet as possible. Don't put yourself where you can hear a clock chime or tick. Breathe deeply and allow your body to relax with each exhalation. As your body relaxes, allow your eyes to close. With your eyes closed, continue breathing deeply.

Exercise
Imagine yourself resting comfortably at home when the postman delivers a medium-sized package. You pick up the package and unwrap it. Inside, nestled in tissue paper, you discover two small bottles.

You examine the label on the first bottle. The label tells you that the liquid inside will remove you from elapsed time for a day. If you drink the liquid, life will go on around you, but you can wish yourself to go anywhere in the world instantly and do anything you please for a period of twenty-four hours.

Now open the bottle and drink the contents. The liquid is warm and bubbly. Swish it around in your mouth, enjoying the texture and taste, and then swallow and feel it pass down your throat. The liquid fills your stomach with a comforting sensation, and you feel pleasantly drowsy. You allow your head to grow heavy and sleepy. The magic potion carries you off into a restful sleep.

When you wake up you are "out of time." No one can see you, but you can operate in the world and affect it. For instance, if you take something away from someone, it will disappear into your time frame and reality. You may wish yourself anywhere in the world and instantly you will be there. You have twenty-four hours to go where you like, see what you wish, and do what you please.

Now take time to imagine what you would like to do.

[*Pause for several minutes*]

Assuming you are sufficiently rested from your first foray out of time, turn to the second magic bottle. The label tells you that this liquid is even more potent than the first. If you should drink it, all activity on the planet Earth will cease for twenty-four hours. Every other human, animal, and piece of machinery will freeze while you are free to pass among them.

Once again you will have the power of wish-travel. For twenty-four hours you may instantly go wherever you please. If you want to, you can bring other people into your time frame the way you did before with objects. They will stay in your time frame only as long as you touch them and actively desire their presence. Once you break contact they will return to suspended animation with the rest of the world.

Pick up the bottle, open it, and drink the magic contents. The liquid is sweet and thick, and you savor it as it passes through your mouth, down your throat, and settles firmly in your stomach. Your head grows heavy and you allow yourself to drift off to sleep.

When you wake up, the world has ground to a halt. You, however, are free to travel wherever you like, and change things to suit you. What will you do to improve your life? What will you do to change the course of history from this day forward? You consider your fondest desires and then proceed to enact them.

[*Pause for several minutes*]

Once you are finished with your day of work, totally relax, breathe deeply, and at the count of three, exhale and open your eyes. One . . . Two . . . Three.

Questions for reflection

How did you feel when you read the label and realized you would be able to stop time? Were you excited or did you have any misgivings?

After drinking from the first bottle, where did you go and what did you do?

Did you feel that twenty-four hours was sufficient time to do what you wanted?

After drinking from the second bottle, where did you go and what did you do?

Looking over both exercises, what changes did you want to see in the world? Do you feel they are occurring at all right now?

Since you cannot stop time in real life, you do not have the power to effect the instant changes you made in this image. On the other hand, you could begin to work on them slowly and steadily. Ask yourself, "What small adjustments in my life's schedule could I make to help bring about these momentous changes?" You have far more than twenty-four hours left within your lifetime, and the added advantage of choosing to work with others on your process of growth and development. What might you do?

Relationship-directed images

These exercises center on your relationships with parents, friends, and lovers to help you gain a better understanding of these people and enhance the quality of your relationships with them.

Parents   p. 114

We can choose our friends, lovers, and associates, but we can't choose our parents. For better or for worse, we are stuck with the parent or parents who raised us. In this two-part exercise you will have an opportunity to assess what you like and dislike about one of the people who raised you, and at the same time, discover which of their qualities you've inherited.

Long lost confidant   p. 120

In this exercise, you will imagine the return of a long lost friend so that you may share with him or her your triumphs and trials. Through this process, you may learn more about yourself as well as about what that other person still means to you.

Party of lifelong friends   p. 126

As we go through stages in our lives, we usually develop several different groups of friends. Travel, education, job changes, break-ups, fallings-out, and death can all affect our circle of friends. In this exercise you are going to imagine inviting all the people you ever liked, including relatives, to a party where you can see them all at their best and give them an opportunity to meet one another.

Loss   p. 131

While we may acknowledge that during our lifetime we will experience a loss, we often avoid thinking about or preparing for it. We ignore the inevitable loss until the moment it happens. When we do experience the loss of someone dear, we may feel frustration, anger, and guilt, which can overwhelm us. This exercise prepares you for a great loss by having you visualize the event prior to its occurrence. What you experience in this image may help you deal more effectively with your emotions during a real loss.

Sex role reversal   p. 134

In this image you will have the opportunity to experience life in the body of someone of the opposite sex. You will choose your sexual counterpart and imagine a typical day in his or her life. The experience may provide extra perspective, appreciation, and insight into your beliefs and biases. Your feelings about the opposite sex may be reinforced, or you may discover some new attitudes and perspectives.

Video will   p. 140

In this exercise, you will videotape your last will and testament, including any thoughts, feelings, and suggestions you want to share with others after you are dead. This will be your opportunity to be totally honest with people about your feelings because you will be beyond their reach.

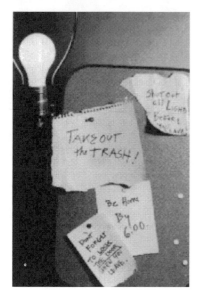

Parents

We can choose our friends, lovers, and associates, but we can't choose our parents. For better or for worse, we are stuck with the parent or parents who raised us. In this two-part exercise you will have an opportunity to assess what you like and dislike about one of the people who raised you, and at the same time, discover which of their qualities you've inherited.

Preparation

In a relaxed and comfortable setting, close your eyes and begin to breathe slowly. On your third exhalation, imagine a room divided in half by a one-way mirror through which, undetected, you can watch the other half of the room. Your presence will be totally unknown by anyone on the other side.

If at any time you start to feel tense or frustrated, know that you can freeze or stop the image. If what you see disturbs you too much, just switch off the light in the other half of the room until you feel calm again.

Now imagine one of the people who was responsible for raising you. Focus your attention on that person's appearance and voice. Think about clothing, gestures, characteristic smell, eyeglasses, or jewelry—anything that made that person distinct.

Exercise
Part 1

Imagine sitting behind the one-way mirror. Across from you, on the other side, is your parent. Before you switch on the light on their side, think about the attributes of this person that bother you: any mannerisms or quirks that you find irritating.

Now, as you switch on the light in the other half of the room, you will see your parent do these annoying things. Watch the scene carefully and think about why these actions bother you.

Remember, you can freeze the image or turn off the light if you become uncomfortable. Also, keep in mind that the other person cannot see or hear you.

While you are studying your parent's annoying habits, you may wish to consider how your parent may feel about these habits. Perhaps your parent is unaware of them, or really needs to behave in these ways. Even if your parent's quirks annoy you, he or she may have a reason for keeping these mannerisms.

[*Pause*]

Now switch off the light and think of someone who does not have these irritating mannerisms. Consider how you feel about this other person. If you can think of other annoying quirks that your parent has, allow yourself to view these mannerisms through the mirror and then focus on another person who does not have these habits. Then switch off the light again.

[*Pause*]

This time, choose some aspects of your parent that you actively dislike. If you have difficulty, you might recall a specific occasion that aroused your anger or disapproval.

When you are ready, switch on the light. Through the one-way mirror, you observe your parent's behavior or the event that angered you. Concentrate on the aspects that you find most upsetting. See if you can imagine your parent's motivations, and remain intensely aware of your feelings as you view this. If you feel like shouting or doing something physical while watching, go ahead. Remember, you cannot be seen or heard.

[*Pause*]

Once you have finished observing, switch off the light. Allow yourself to relax again. Then think of someone who would not have done what you have just seen. Perhaps it's just not in that other person's character, you cannot imagine it, or you know this other person would have behaved differently. Contrast this individual with your parent and identify how you feel about the differences.

When you have compared these two people to your satisfaction, open your eyes and return to the present. Evaluate what you have observed and felt while looking through the mirror.

Questions for reflection

At what point in each of these scenes did you feel your anger rise? What did you feel like doing?

Did you have any negative feelings?

Who did you choose to compare with your parent?

Once you compared them, how did you feel about your parent lacking the other person's qualities?

Looking back at these qualities that annoyed or upset you, can you see any of them in yourself? If you cannot, why do you think your parent has them? How did you avoid them?

What do you think your parent might have to give up in order to acquire the characteristics you desire him or her to have?

Is it possible that the annoying quirks are trivial enough for you to accept?

Did you learn anything new about yourself while you watched these events through the mirror?

Part 2
Now imagine you are sitting before the one-way mirror again, but the other half of the room is in darkness. You are going to think about the little quirks and manner- isms in your parent's behavior that you like. These are habits that give you pleasure and evoke warm feelings towards this person who has taken care of you.

If you think of a specific incident that was especially pleasant and would like to see it, switch on the light beyond the glass. There you can see your parent in the scene that made you feel good. Concentrate on the details that gave you the most pleasure: a certain movement, a sound, a remark, an aroma.

If you remember a number of pleasant mannerisms and would enjoy seeing them again, take all the time you need to watch this person perform them on the other side of the mirror. Be sure to notice your feelings as you watch. When you have viewed these pleasant actions to your satisfaction, switch off the light.

[*Pause*]

Finally, select those aspects of your parent's behavior that you love. Perhaps there are characteristic things your parent does often. Perhaps you can recall specific experiences with this person that were particularly wonderful. Maybe you remember something he or she said to you.

As you add up these lovable items, you may desire to view them through the one-way mirror. If you do, switch on the light and watch your parent in action. Remain aware of your emotions as you view your parent and think about what this behavior meant to you at the time—and what it means to you now.

After you've spent some time viewing the behaviors you love about your parent, switch off the light one last time.

Keeping the positive emotions alive, focus your attention on your breathing—calm and full. Count three full breaths and when you get to three, open your eyes.

Questions for reflection

Do you feel you have inherited any of this parent's pleasant mannerisms? Do you find that other people respond positively to these mannerisms in you?

At what point did your parent's actions fill you with love or appreciation?

What did you learn about yourself from this exercise? If you feel you do not have your parent's pleasant habits, why do you think this is so?

How did you feel about working with parts one and two of this image? Was one part easier than the other? Why?

Did you learn anything new about this parent? What about yourself?

Now that you have this information about what you like and dislike about this parent, which of the following courses of action can you take: help them to understand what you like and dislike, help yourself to accept what you feel, or help both of you work on your mutual feelings?

Note: Since this exercise focuses on only one parent, you may want to experience it again for your other parent or for anyone else who helped raise you.

Long lost confidant

Each of us encounters key people who play an important role in our growth. Through the twists and turns of time and fate, we may lose touch with some of these special people. At times we may wish a special person from our past were here today. Perhaps that other person knew our aspirations and would have wanted to know about the events that have occurred since our separation. In this exercise, you will imagine the return of a long lost friend so that you may share with him or her your triumphs and trials. Through this process, you may learn more about yourself as well as about what that other person still means to you.

Preparation
Make yourself comfortable at home. If you have photos or other memorabilia to jog your memory, take them out and examine them. Now think of someone who meant a lot to you, someone you have lost all contact with and are not likely to see again. This person might be deceased, a childhood friend, or a close relationship you once had. Once you have a vivid picture of this special person, close your eyes, and begin.

Exercise
While you have been concentrating, your surroundings have become a scientific research center. You are in a large modern room. The walls are shiny metal. You see

a technician standing by a panel with various-colored buttons and lights on it. Two chairs, surrounded by large, clear cylinders, sit in the far end of the room.

The technician walks over to you and explains that within this room is a miracle of modern technology. This technological advance will allow you to bridge the gaps of time and space so that you can meet with a person you haven't seen in many years. You need only step into the first cylinder and think of this person and he or she will be transported from your mind into the second cylinder.

The technician explains that you must not make any sudden moves or loud noises, because the energy field will be disturbed and the visit terminated. If all goes well, however, you should be able to touch and talk with your friend. Once the two of you have been reacquainted to your satisfaction, the machine will then project your mental images onto a screen for your friend to see. In this way, your long-lost intimate friend will be able to learn about the significant events of your life since the time the two of you parted.

The technician asks, "Are you ready?" You prepare yourself for a moment, examining your feelings about the imminent arrival of this old companion. Stepping up to one of the cylinders, you walk through the doorway held open by the technician and sit down on the chair. Tell the technician you are ready.

Sitting in the chair, you close your eyes and begin to concentrate on the memory of that special person. You hear a hum increasing around you. The floor vibrates just a little. As you open your eyes and look at the dark cylinder across from you, you notice a slight mist forming inside there. Gradually this mist draws to-gether over the seat of the chair.

You strain your eyes to see what is happening, and slowly the image of a person begins to form in the other cylinder. As the mist clears, you can see your friend, and you realize that the person has actually returned.

Now that this person is before you, sort through all your feelings. Look at one another. Show each other that you understand. Assign no guilt or blame because of your separation. The past no longer matters; you are together now.

Gaze at your friend's face, take in the features and note any changes. What does this face suggest to you? What can it tell you about the experiences your friend has had? Through his or her expressions, your friend is looking at you and getting his or her own sense of the changes that are apparent in your face.

You feel the urge to reach out and touch, to make contact. You find that through your desire, emotions, and will, the glass cylinder is gone. You can touch, shake hands, and embrace.

Out of the corner of your eye, you notice the technician pushing a button that lowers a huge white screen in front of the two of you. This screen will allow you to share what has happened to you since you last saw your friend.

With the screen now down, the two of you return to your chairs and push them close together. You explain to your friend what is about to transpire. Experiences that are special and sacred to you will now be shared.

Career moves, new friends, achievements, and even setbacks are depicted on the screen. You show your friend everything you might have wished to share at the time it happened. As the movie progresses, you glance over at your companion from time to time to observe his or her reactions.

[*Pause*]

You take all the time you need to show your friend all you want. Eventually the story arrives at the circumstances of the present. You realize that you have shared everything you wanted your friend to know.

You look deeply into your friend's eyes. The message there, beyond all words, is clear: *I have experienced all your thoughts and the events of your life. I am glad you could share them with me, and I understand where you are now. This has meant much to me. Now I am ready to go.*

The two of you exchange a few warm farewells. You push your chairs back to their original spots. By the time you have sat down again, you realize that the cylinders are back in place.

Gazing at your friend, you hear the humming intensify. A mist gathers in the other cylinder, making it difficult to see. You wave good-bye to your departing confidant and close your eyes. The noise and vibrations pick up and then subside.

When you open your eyes, you see that the cylinders and the other chair are gone. The technician is standing near you. He congratulates you for having experienced a successful visitation. He then asks you to settle into the chair and close your eyes.

He says, "Allow your eyes to shut and meditate upon this wonderful experience. You have had a fantastic opportunity to bring a long lost friend up to date on your activities. A feeling of peace and contentment comes over you. When you open your eyes, you will be home and in familiar surroundings."

Open your eyes and find yourself at home again. In front of you is the photograph of your long-lost confidant. Perhaps you can detect a hint of warmth and contentment in that face because the person has seen you again. Also, you know that you can visit your friend in the laboratory any time you choose.

Questions for reflection

How did you feel when you realized that you would come face to face with your long lost friend once again? What were your feelings prior to informing the technician that you were ready?

How did you feel when you actually saw your friend?

By looking closely at your friend, what changes could you detect in his or her face? What changes do you believe your friend saw in you?

Did you touch your companion? What was your reaction?

Which experiences were most important to share with this other person?

Did you sense any strong reactions in your companion as he or she watched your life experiences on the screen?

Were you conscious of anything you chose not to put before your companion?

How did you feel having shared your life experiences with this other person?

If you could have this experience with other people you have lost over time, whom would you choose and why? What do you feel you have gained from this exercise?

As we go through stages in our lives, we usually develop several different groups of friends. Travel, education, job changes, break-ups, falling-outs, and death can all affect our circle of friends. In this exercise you are going to imagine inviting all the people you ever liked, including relatives, to a party where you can see them all at their best and give them an opportunity to meet one another.

Party of lifelong friends

Preparation
Make an inventory of your lifetime acquaintances. Look at scrapbooks, photo albums, and yearbooks to help jog your memories. If you come across old friends with whom you've had a falling out, or lovers you no longer go out with, try and recall them as they were when you were closest to them.

Put the photographs of your friends and family in chronological order and study their faces one at a time. Once you have studied all their faces, go back to the first one and make a second trip through the collection, allowing memories to enter your mind as they occur to you. As you near the end of the chronology a second time, shut your eyes and imagine yourself standing in a big empty banquet hall a few hours before a party.

Exercise
You are making final arrangements for the party. This large hall will be filled with all your invited guests. At

the moment it is being cleared in preparation for the tables and decorations.

The hall manager asks you to go over the checklist with her. "Approximately how many people will be here," she asks. You do some swift calculations and quote a number. She asks you to take a long moment to consider any special features you wish to include. You review your preferences in decor, food, and music. At this point you can make any arrangements you want for the perfect atmosphere for your party.

Once you are fairly comfortable with the details, you go home to get showered and dressed. The party is at eight, and it's five o'clock now: time to decide what to wear. You carefully consider the outfit that will best express the person you are today.

Later, when you arrive at the hall, it is already filled with people. You are going to have the opportunity to mingle, observe, catch up on old friends, and talk to whomever you wish. As you visit with people, try to remain aware of your feelings.

Near the door stands a clique of people you admired when you were small. Go up to them and notice that their eyes light up when they see you. Converse with them about the changes you've experienced in the intervening years.

Further into the hall are your favorite relatives, past and present. It's a pleasure to see them all together here, unaccompanied by other relations with whom you may not have been as close. They thank you for inviting them and chat about your present activities.

It's amazing to glance around the hall and see so many people—all people that you know—gathered in one place. They all came!

Nearby is a person you had a crush on in school. You wander over and learn to your pleasure that this person had always liked your personality and wanted to know you better.

To your right is a group of people you've met through work. They express surprise to see so many people from other facets of your life, facets to which they had never been exposed. It's pleasant conversing with these people about things other than work.

Once you've had a chance to touch base with everyone, drift to one side and watch the others interact. Here is a collection of people from every period in your life: childhood, school days, and work. Some you may have wanted to introduce to one another before because you had a hunch they'd get along. Others you might never have imagined together. Spend some time watching them converse.

Of course, they all have their experiences with you in common, and many of the conversations going on in the hall do concern you—occasionally you catch an appreciative glance in your direction—but mostly these wonderful people are taking this opportunity to share with each other. You notice several of them exchange phone numbers and addresses.

Finally, a few guests begin to say their farewells. The party has been a great success, but the hour is late. Everyone thanks you for a great time, and a couple of people say they'd like to have one of their own.

The party winds down and you say your good-byes. Still primed by the excitement of the evening, you make your way home and pull out a photo album to look at the faces of some of the people you have just seen. As you glance through the pages, your eyelids grow heavy and you drift into a full and relaxing sleep.

On the count of three you will wake up fully rested and relaxed, returning to the room with the photos of some wonderful people in front of you.
One . . . Two . . . Three.

Questions for reflection

Did the prospect of a party of lifetime friends excite you?

Did you have any apprehensions about having so many people together in one place?

What sort of effect did you intend the food, music, and decor to have?

What effect did you intend your outfit to have?

How did you feel when you saw the hall full of people? Were you surprised at the number?

Party of lifelong friends

How many different kinds of friends have you had? What aspects of your personality did they bring out? What needs did they meet at the time you knew them?

How well did your different sets of friends interact with one another? Did you imagine any particular people getting along especially well?

Were there any individuals or groups who did not seem to get along with the others? If so, why?

How did you feel as the party wound down? Would you ever like to have a real party like this?

Looking back, do you feel there is any type of friend that would have been good for you, that you did not meet and could not have invited to the party?

Can you gauge the impact you had on all these people's lives?

While we may acknowledge that during our lifetime we will experience a loss, we often avoid thinking about or preparing for it. We ignore the inevitable loss until the moment it happens. When we do experience the loss of someone dear, we may feel frustration, anger, and guilt, which can overwhelm us.

The following exercise prepares you for a great loss by having you visualize the event prior to its occurrence. What you experience in this image may help you deal more effectively with your emotions during a real loss.

Loss

Preparation
Put yourself in a warm, comfortable setting. Practice your relaxation techniques and close your eyes. Choose one of the most precious people in your life today for this exercise.

Exercise
As you continue to relax, think about this person's appearance. Recall the good and happy times you've had together—experiences shared, projects tackled, as well as struggles undergone together. Think about your feelings for this person—where you believe your relationship now stands, and where you would like it to be.

The phone rings. When you pick up the receiver, a voice tells you that this precious person has passed away.

Without waiting for the details, replace the receiver and ponder your feelings. The person who meant so much to you is gone: no advance warning, no farewells, and no further opportunities to be together. Think about how you feel, keeping as calm as possible.

How do you feel? Why do you think you feel this way? Do you feel any guilt? Are there things you have lost the opportunity to say or do? Have you said or done anything that may have hurt this person? What emotions do you feel? Why do you feel them, and where are they directed?

Is there anything you can now do to alleviate these powerful feelings? More importantly, do you think you could have done anything in advance to soften these emotions?

[*Pause*]

Now that you have thought about the possibility of your loved one's death realize that you have not yet lost him or her. You have only been imagining that loss. Focus on your present relationship with this person. Take another moment or two to recognize what you have been feeling, and on a count of three, allow yourself to awaken refreshed and alert. One . . . Two . . . Three.

Questions for reflection

Was it easy or difficult to imagine the loss? Were your emotions overwhelming?

What mixture of emotions—positive and negative—did you experience after visualizing the loss of this special person?

Have you thought about how other people's lives would be affected by this loss? Who in particular? What might you do with them?

Now that you realize you have not lost this person, what steps could you take to avoid future anger, guilt, or pain?

Do you think you will use your experiences in this exercise as an opportunity to do something now, or will you put it off as you have in the past?

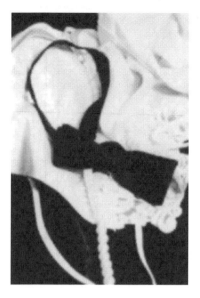

Sex role reversal

One of the most universal themes throughout history has been the lack of understanding between the sexes. People tend to deal with their confusion either by treating members of the opposite sex with adoration or denigration. The tremendous preoccupation with this issue is reflected in the vast and growing literature on gender identity, sexuality, and changing roles in our society.

In this image you will have the opportunity to experience life in the body of someone of the opposite sex. You will choose your sexual counterpart and imagine a typical day in his or her life. The experience may provide extra perspective, appreciation, and insight into your beliefs and biases. Your feelings about the opposite sex may be reinforced, or you may discover some new attitudes and perspectives.

Preparation
Find a photograph of some unknown person who looks similar to you in many ways but is your sexual opposite. While inhaling and exhaling slowly and deeply, stare at the picture for a minute or two. Then close your eyes and visualize the person in the picture as best you can. Open your eyes and stare at the photograph again, taking in the person's every feature. Then close your eyes a second time and remember what this person looks like. Mentally re-create an image of the person. Open your eyes one final time and stare at the picture again to solidify that image in your memory. Once you have a clear image of the person, close your eyes, and begin.

Exercise

Imagine that you are just coming out of a deep and restful sleep in a luxurious bed. You are on vacation in a part of the country where there are many people, but no one knows you. As you lie there half awake between the warm sheets, you look around your elegant hotel room.

When you sit up in bed and notice yourself in the mirror across the room, you realize you have a new sexual identity. The person you see in the mirror, the person you *are*, is your sexual opposite. Take a moment to think about what this means, and how it feels to inhabit this new body. Do you feel any emotions associated with this change?

Get up from the bed, stretch, and wander over to the full-length mirror. Take an inventory of your new body. Explore what it feels like on a physical level. Take note of the differences. Examine your hair, the texture of your skin, your arms, legs, muscle tone, breasts, and genitals. Notice what feels different under your touch, and your reactions to these differences in you.

Now that you've examined your body, you prepare to go down to breakfast. Consider what clothing you are going to wear and what effect you wish to achieve. Then feel yourself putting on these articles of clothing. Your underclothes may be entirely different, and you should take note of how they feel against your skin. Your outer clothes may enclose your body in new ways—they feel tight and loose in places that are different from those you have known in the past. Be aware of all this.

If there is anything you wish to do to your face to

freshen it, go to the bathroom and do it. Decide whether there are any extra adornments you want to include and what sort of trouble you might like to take with your hair. Once dressed, take a good look at yourself in the mirror and see the image you project. If you see anything you want to change or emphasize, do it now.

You are going to eat breakfast in the hotel restaurant. As you walk down the hall, ride the elevator, and make your way to the dining area, notice the people you pass. Observe the way they walk and the way they look at you—whether they hold your glance, drop their eyes, or tend to stare at some part of you other than your face. Also notice what you focus on in other people.

The maitre d' is waiting at the entrance to the hotel restaurant. He asks how many are in your party and you indicate that you will be dining alone. See how he reacts to your comment, if at all, as he leads you to a table.

Once you are seated, scan the menu and order breakfast. Think carefully about how this new you might dine, what foods and what amounts you would order. While you wait for breakfast, glance at the other hotel diners. Observe how they interact with one another, and note the expressions on their faces if they catch your eye.

A waiter brings your food. While you eat, plan out your day. How does a person of your sex and character spend a vacation day in a strange city? What sights would you want to see, and how would you be likely to spend vacation money? Can you foresee any discomfort in being alone in an unknown place? Would you prefer to hook up with a tour group?

Plan out an entire day for yourself, and try to remain aware of what choices you make differently because of your new body.

[*Pause*]

You are back in the hotel restaurant, but it is the evening of your long vacation day and you are waiting for dinner. At a nearby table you notice another solitary diner, and you think it would be nice to have someone to talk with. This other person notices you, too. Decide whether you can ask this stranger to join you for dinner or whether you should wait to be asked.

Once you are seated at the same table as the attractive stranger, imagine your conversation. Create a plausible life for yourself: describe your work, your childhood, your interests, your ambitions. Make sure all the details are in keeping with a person of your character and sex. Watch your dinner companion's face to see how all these details are taken.

You notice that your dinner date finds you attractive. The two of you have had an enjoyable meal together. You have a very good feeling about your day and the dinner, and yet when your new acquaintance asks to come up to your room, you are confused.

Perhaps this is going too far. Perhaps it is a little too fast, especially when you have a week of vacation to spend in this city. In any case, you are not entirely ready to invite a guest into your hotel room. You must find a way to tell this to your new friend without causing hurt feelings. Think carefully about an effective reply, then say it.

Watch your companion's face closely. See if further explanation is necessary. Once you feel you have adequately explained your position, decide how the two of you are going to handle the dinner bill. As soon as it is paid, take your leave and return to your room alone.

Disrobing is a pleasant experience. Notice what you have to do to remove all the clothing you have worn today, and how it feels to do so. Do whatever things you must at the sink in order to prepare for sleep. Before getting into bed, stand at the window and look at the twinkling lights of the city. Think of the wonderful things you did today and decide what you would like to do (or avoid) tomorrow.

Now prepare to open your eyes and return to the room you started this exercise in. On the count of three you will wake up and be back in your own body. One . . . Two . . . Three.

Questions for reflection

Did you find it easy or difficult to locate a picture of someone you would consider your sexual counterpart?

Did the person you chose possibly have better attributes than your true sexual counterpart would have? What were they?

How did it feel to possess this wholly new and different body? Was it hard to imagine?

What pleased you most about your new physical appearance? What did you find least appealing?

What stood out as being most different in your clothing, facial preparation, and extra accoutrements?

How would you describe the image you projected?

What, if anything, was different about your vacation activities from your normal choices?

Did you concoct a background that was similar to your actual one, or did you make up something radically different?

Throughout the day, how did people treat you differently from the way you are used to being treated in real life? Was their behavior toward you entirely pleasant for you, or did any of it make you uncomfortable?

What was it like to decline the intimate invitation from your dinner date?

How did the two of you pay for your dinner? What factors influenced the decision you arrived at?

Video will

In this exercise, you will videotape your last will and testament, including any thoughts, feelings, and suggestions you want to share with others after you are gone. This will be your opportunity to be totally honest with everyone about your feelings because you will be beyond their reach.

Because this exercise focuses on death, and feelings of guilt, anger, or regret that may go with it, it can be emotionally charged for some people.

Preparation

On a sheet of paper make two lists—one of all your valued possessions, the other of all the people in your life. Then decide how to divide your property. You don't have to earmark every trinket, but take care of this business in a general way before you start the exercise.

Next, put an X by the people on your list for whom you have criticisms. Although you may not wish to leave them anything, it is possible that they will attend your funeral and the playing of your will, which will give you the opportunity to express your true feelings and settle old scores. Remember, this message will be in your will, so nothing you say can come back to hurt you.

Once you have drawn up this checklist, close your eyes, relax, and imagine that you have passed away.

Exercise

The people you know or knew in your lifetime have gathered together in a large drawing room. They are talking quietly among themselves, and waiting. Finally, a door opens and a lawyer steps in and calls for silence.

"The deceased had a lot to say about the division of the estate," the lawyer tells the assembled group. "In addition, the deceased wanted to make a number of statements to and about many of you here. Through the vehicle of video technology, you will now be able to see your departed loved one speak to you directly."

In response to this news, there is some murmuring and a nervous chuckle or two. Several people make appreciative sounds while others shift in their seats. The lawyer steps over to the VCR and turns it on.

Allow yourself to appear before the audience of friends and associates. You are going to speak to them from a screen beyond their reach. You have the opportunity to say everything you always wanted to say, and none of them can reach you, either emotionally or physically, to hurt or to hug.

The first thing you can do is thank them all for coming. Although your audience might feel strange about listening to and seeing you after you've passed away, this is the best way to communicate all you have to say.

Focus your attention upon the individuals next to whose names you have placed an X. Some of them may not be in attendance because your relationship with them was less than favorable, but you may address them anyway. Someone may pass the word on to them, and your loved ones might appreciate the opportunity to learn your true feelings about these people.

Take the time to speak to each of these persons. Tell

them how you really feel about them. Perhaps you would be willing to give them a small piece of the estate if they change their behavior or attitude in some way. If you have any lasting words of wisdom, any advice about what they might do with their lives based on your knowledge of them, leave them with that.

[*Pause to address these people*]

Once you have spoken to all the people with an X, the lawyer dismisses them. "You may leave," he tells them. "If you have any further questions, get in touch with me later." As soon as those people have left, you can begin to explain what will be done with your estate. If you wish to bequeath anything to charities or institutions, you instruct the lawyer accordingly.

[*Pause*]

Now you are ready to divide up the remaining property among your business associates, relations, and friends. As you do, you will address each person and explain the reasons for your choice of gift, as well as your feelings and advice for the recipient.

The first group comprises your business associates, mentors, and teachers. You explain to them what they taught you, what they stood for, and why they were important and special to you. Then you specify which item or items from your estate will go to them.

[*Pause*]

The second group includes distant relatives, friends, and business partners. These are all people with whom you have had cordial, warm, and even enjoyable relations. With each person you recount the good experiences, the funny times, and the role the person played in your life. After indicating the possessions that will go to all of them, include a few words about their future: you wish them all the best, and you hope they live their lives to the fullest.

[*Pause*]

The final group you address comprises your intimate circle of loved ones: perhaps your spouse, or lover; brothers, sisters, children, or parents. These are the people who gave the most meaning to your life and in whose lives you undoubtedly played a crucial role.

Explain what you are giving to each one and the reasons. Sometimes the tiny possessions that hold enormous personal significance and memories mean more than objects of immense monetary value. Tell each person how much he or she has meant to you, and how different your life might have been if your paths had never crossed.

Perhaps you have something important to tell them that you never shared when you were alive. This is your chance to share without holding back, to make a true confession, to cleanse your soul of whatever emotions you wish—and to leave these wonderful people with a more complete understanding of your life and your feelings for them.

[*Pause*]

There is a final piece of business before you say fare-well. You express your wishes for what you want done with your body. Once you have done that, you thank the lawyer for his help in arranging this unique gathering, and then you say good-bye to the assembled group. Many faces have tears running down them, but many have smiles of love as well. You have an immensely satisfying sensation of relief at a job well done.

As you watch the people file out of the room, knowing their heads are filled with what you said to them, you realize that this was only a rehearsal. You are not dead. In fact, you are very much alive, and in a moment you will awaken to reflect upon this remarkable experience. Focus now on your breathing. As you become more aware of each breath, your body begins to awaken and you gradually return to a full state of consciousness. Now open your eyes and reflect on this exercise.

Questions for reflection

How did you feel about this opportunity to speak to people honestly in this one-way interaction?

What sort of remarks did you address to the people whose names had an X? Was it pleasant talking to them in this manner, or was it difficult? Did you notice any signs of surprise or anger in their faces?

Was there a better way to say the things you said to the people with X's, and could you share these same thoughts with them face-to-face?

Did the exercise make you feel more comfortable and motivated to speak honestly with these people now, while you're still alive?

What gifts from your estate seemed to have the greatest effect on their recipients?

When you spoke to your mentors, relatives, and loved ones, did you find yourself making evaluations of your relationship with them that you had not made before?

Do you think any of the nice things you had to say to people would come as a surprise to them if you told them today? Would you like to tell them?

Was this an entirely satisfying exercise, or was any part painful?

Do you think it might be worthwhile now to give away some of the gifts you imagined bequeathing after your death?

Conclusion

I wish to congratulate you for experiencing the imagery exercises in this book. It takes a lot of courage to attempt this sort of self-exploration. You have taken the time to explore the facets of your personality, your memory, and many potential areas of change, and have, hopefully, grown and profited from these experiences. I hope you have a feeling of accomplishment, and with it, a sense of well-being. Perhaps you feel better about the person you have discovered yourself to be. However, don't be surprised if some of the things you have uncovered seem unresolved, or are still puzzling to you. Although you might have read every preceding page and experienced every image, your journey has just begun, and these exercises can still help you on your way. You can return to them later for greater insight and further growth because, in a sense, you will be a different person tomorrow, next month, and next year.

I hope you'll use this book as an ongoing reference. Perhaps you will want to earmark certain images that spoke most effectively to your problems and concerns. Also, if you had a smooth run through an image and nothing particularly interesting happened, don't assume you won't have any use for it in the future. You may find that some powerful images go stale as you work through your growth with them, and that others which seemed to have nothing to say to you in one phase of your life become potent with time.

Appendix

A brief history of imagery

Some of the oldest physical evidence of humankind's presence on earth is believed to be examples of visualization. Based on observations of modern-day hunting tribes in Africa, anthropologists theorize that Cro-Magnon cave paintings of animals were meant to aid men in preparing for the hunt. To draw the animal was to capture its soul. Throwing spears at the animals pictured on the walls was akin to spearing them in the flesh. The inner image and the outer reality were inseparably linked, and what took place symbolically would naturally affect the material world.

Our ancestors appear to have related to the world very differently from the way we do. To them, spirits and the imagination were merely another plane of the same reality. Even today, in the cult of voodoo in Haiti, people believe that the image of the object and its reality are linked. A doll or puppet image of a person in the hands of an enemy can bring about illness, pain, or even death. Believing implicitly in the potency of images, people can be convinced of their reality.

In industrialized nations, we are encouraged to maintain a sharp line between the imagination and the physical world. Most adults believe that imagination can have no affect on physical events, but children, even in sophisticated cultures, still cross that line. Imaginary playmates, monsters under the bed or in the closet, pets and toys that talk, the tooth fairy, and Santa Claus are important, accepted parts of childhood. Since we are all born with the basic equipment to imagine and visualize, the change comes from a cultural evolution, not a physical one. Although there are many reasons for the ascent of the tangible, one of the first steps may have been the development of written language.

As the Chinese alphabet clearly illustrates, many written symbols began as a direct depiction of the images they represented. The Chinese ideogram for house is a stylized two-dimensional image of a simple house: two parallel vertical lines with a horizontal line crossing them. Words were meant to make you see the images—to enable people to visualize over long distances and across time. Writing enabled people to keep records without having to depend on the fallible memories of storytellers or the longevity of a village wiseman or woman.

Eventually, people paid less attention to remembering details, since writing substituted so effectively for cultural and historical memory. Instead of being the living manifestation of the images they represented, words evolved into abstractions, a means of objectifying experience and proving the reality and truth of a statement.

Although this change to written language is considered to be a positive one, it has had a profound effect on what is expected of individuals in a scientifically-oriented culture. There are very few arenas where it is defensible to accept anything on faith, or on the unproven word of another person. What goes on in the human mind is a matter of cells, synapses, and chemicals, and seeing something that isn't provably there is seen as a sign of illness or chemical dependency. "Making things up" is not encouraged by most of our educational systems, or by parents of children beyond the age of six.

Society has discouraged people from communicating with their non-concrete sides. Both the Old and the New Testament are filled with stories of dreams and visions: from Jacob's ladder to the prophet Ezekiel to Jesus being tempted by Satan. Yet most contemporary Christian churches are either skeptical or derisive of people who claim to have experienced miracles or visions, although all religions have at their roots a belief in things that cannot be objectively proven. After all, even true believers must live in a world where photographs can be taken, and hoaxes easily unveiled.

Jewish mysticism, a rich and complex vein, is generally

mined now only for its historical and cultural aspects. Eastern religions, many of which still maintain their connections to their visionary roots, are studied in the West for their philosophy but treated as cults when their ideas gain converts here.

Despite institutionalized disapproval, there is ample documentation of the importance of imagery in the creative process. Ironically, some important cultural and philosophical milestones in Western culture may have been the product of non-Western, non-linear thinking. English poet and illustrator William Blake created his entire body of work from the images of his inner world. Nietzsche claimed that the body of work which became *Thus Spake Zarathustra* originated in daydreams. When questioned about his methods, Einstein stated that he seldom thought in words at all, and conceived of the concept of relativity while imagining himself on a beam traveling at the speed of light. Mozart spoke of imagining his compositions as complete and finished pieces. He could sit back and listen to them being played by his mental orchestra, and would simply transcribe what he heard.

Psychology, because it is the study of our inner worlds, is the only nonreligious school of thought which continues to use imagery as a tool. Yet even psychology has evolved in its attitude toward imagery.

The discipline of psychology was born amid the nineteenth-century explosion of Western scientific and technical knowledge. The heart of nineteenth-century scientific method was the assumption that the observed is real. Even worlds of the past left their quantifiable signatures. Imagination was the province of poets, not serious professionals. Freud's theories, despite the fact that they were based on serious clinical observations, shocked the scientific community because they reintroduced the concept of relative reality, that our internal perceptions affect our external realities.

Freud was led to his theories and techniques because, as a neurologist, he was often confronted with cases of hysterical medical disorders. Called upon to treat a woman whose arm appeared paralyzed, he could find no observable medical reason for the condition. And yet, the patient was obviously not faking her ailment. Slowly, he began to see that she, and other people like her, had created their conditions as a symptom of their emotional difficulties and troubled histories, but were not consciously aware that they had done so. Through trial and error, he developed the techniques of free association and dream analysis that became foundations of psychoanalytic theory. The idea that what you think (at least subconsciously) could have an affect on your corporeal existence had once again surfaced.

Building upon Freud's work, Jung encouraged his clients to use a method he called "active imagination." In essence, this meant a constant monitoring of daydreams and their spontaneous images. It appeared to him that many of the most potent of these images were duplicated in many people and had nothing to do with their ages or backgrounds. Through this work, Jung developed a framework of "archetypal," or universally evocative, symbols that he believed had their roots in a primitive collective unconscious. For example, in both primitive societies and modern ones, he found the bird to be a symbol of freedom and transcendence representing the ability to let go of the material world and transform. This led him, however, to view all dream images as mere personal interpretations of concepts and symbols that were "hard-wired" into our psyches. It also made it necessary to have a trained interpreter analyze dreams for their archetypal significance, and to fit those dreams into some predefined assessment. Moreover, not surprisingly, these assessments were colored by Jung and his followers' cultural and sexual biases.

Imagery-oriented work continued to be done in Europe in the period between the first and second world wars. The French psychotherapist Robert Desoille and his German contemporary J. H. Schultz did related work on therapist-directed daydreaming and the use of guided fantasy. But by the 1920s the prevailing view of psychologists in the United States had begun to turn against imaging as a tool when more emphasis was placed on psychology as a branch of physiology—the study of the body. The scientific method demands quantifiable results, reproducibility, and clear linkages between cause and effect. But in the study of mental imagery, based as it is on the differences between internal and external perceptions, these links are ambiguous. Thus mental imagery does not easily lend itself to proof via the scientific method. In this regard, visualization and guided imagery take a back seat to the two schools of thought that most people tend to identify with psychology—behavior modification (Skinner-type behavior theory) and classic psychoanalysis.

Behavior theory, boiled down to a sentence, postulates that if you make it pleasant to do one thing, and unpleasant to do another, then you can change behavior, cure abnormalities, and develop a predictable, mappable scenario of what an individual is likely to do. Imagery, when considered at all, is primarily a tool in aversion therapy, which is depicted blackly in *A Clockwork Orange,* where the protagonist is made to react negatively to Beethoven. Classic Freudian psychoanalysis, on the other hand, places a great deal of emphasis on words and memory as tools in tracking the specific happenings that affected a person's development, with the assumption that if you can find what triggered the person's unconscious behavior and bring it to their conscious perception, their conscious awareness will enable them to break free of their disturbed behavior and perceptions. In this view, imagery is a psychoanalyst's microscope, letting him view slides of the subconscious and focus them before sharing the results with the patient.

This limited use of imagery began to change in the 1960s, as more and more evidence began to accumulate that the cognitive brain has more than just two states—conscious and unconscious. As more experimentation (controlled and otherwise) was done with hallucinogenic drugs, sensory deprivation and sleep research, it became clear that not all thought manifestations could be explained through either learned response or experiential analysis. Documented evidence began to mount that people without psychotic disorders not only could, but often did, engage in imagery or sensory delusions akin to hallucination. American psychologists, who had leaned heavily toward behaviorism, began to look back toward Europe, where psychologists such as Hans Carl Leuner had never stopped working with imagery. Exciting but no longer controversial, guided imagery again became an acceptable therapeutic practice.

Today, imagery's applications continue to grow as we learn more about our minds and the way we think. Imagery is being used in professional sports as a means of maintaining a positive self-image and optimizing performance. One sports psychologist who consults for a football team has actually been able to influence which rookies survive preseason cuts by working with them during training camp. By visualizing themselves in winning situations on the field, the players actually seem to perform at a higher, more competent level in reality. Imagery works equally well in less competitive situations. Professor Joseph Hart of the University of Arkansas takes clients "into the future" through imagery and helps them experience mental success, which translates into rebuilt confidence and creative solutions to problems in daily life.

No one is surprised when someone who loses a loved one or receives depressing news develops a headache or comes down with the flu. "Their resistance is down" is the folk-wisdom. Yet being able to take positive, curative control of the body has seemed beyond our control. New studies seem to indicate that this may not be so. Some of the most tantalizing potentials for imagery and visualization are still in their infancy, and center around imagery as a tool for gaining control of bodily functions and states that have generally been considered beyond conscious control. For example, visualization and a positive attitude can have more affect on a patient's well-being than pain killers and anti-anxiety pills. California psychiatrist Dr. Louis Gottschalk developed a test to measure the "hope quotient" of cancer patients, and discovered that those with high hope quotients had higher survival rates than those who tested low. Psychologist Janice Kiecolt-Glaser at Ohio State University College of Medicine has conducted experiments with the elderly which offer relaxation training as a tool to enhance their resistance to disease. At the end of the training, those individuals who had taken part in the study showed a significant increase in activity in their immune systems.

Even more provocative experiments seem to point to imagery as a potential tool in the fight against diseases in which the immune system plays a leading role, from lupus to AIDS to some forms of cancer. After putting people under hypnosis, psychologist Howard Hall of Pennsylvania State University suggested to his experimental group that their white blood cells were sharks hunting down and attacking vulnerable germs. As part of the experiment, the subjects went home and practiced creating this image. Many of the people who took part in the experiment showed an increased white blood cell count after the hypnotic sessions, which implies a tangible, measurable response by their immune systems.

Clearly, a renaissance in the study and applications of guided imagery is taking place. From athletic performance to academic achievement, from self-knowledge to self-healing, as we discover more about creativity, dreams, and the complex interrelationship of mind and body, the history of imagery and visualization continues to be written.

Guided imagery and the subconscious

You are a treasure house of collected images. The experiences received by your five senses help form your beliefs and behaviors in ways of which you are seldom aware. The process of living—acting and interacting—constantly changes your collection of habits, patterns, problems, and virtues. As each layer is laid down, more levels of complexity cloud your actions.

As newborns, we relate to the world as a succession of sensory images. Through repetition, infants gradually sort, categorize, and associate feelings with the appearance of people and objects. Through this accumulation of private experiences, infants develop likes and dislikes. For example, based on an infant's prior experiences, the sight and smell of its mother may elicit emotional reactions completely independent from what that mother is doing at the moment.

At some point, as a toddler acquires names for the images he or she has been experiencing directly—like Daddy, cat, or blanket—the complexity of language enters. In a sense, then, words *become* images. For example, once we have a word for cat, the real animal's presence becomes unnecessary for us to "see" it. When someone says "cat," a child can visualize an animal experienced in the past—and the emotions associated with a cat's purring and warm fur, or its claws.

Language makes it easy for us to create new images from old ones. Though we may have seen only black or white cats, we can combine our experiences of *cat* and *blue* in our mind to imagine a blue cat. If someone tells us an exotic food is "like rice, but sweeter and gritty," we can visualize it and judge whether we're willing to eat it.

Underlying language are its emotional roots. We store our early experiences of mother, darkness, hunger, dogs, etc. along with the feelings they evoked. These feelings emerge in response to later experiences with the same or similar objects. If, for example, our youthful experiences with cats were unpleasant, a new animal may continue to evoke fear, dislike, or discomfort even after we have learned that this specific cat is harmless and affectionate.

We often react intensely without knowing why, without even realizing what the triggering event was. For example, we may feel immediate dislike, for no apparent reason, toward someone we just met. Our subconscious may be associating a hair style, voice, or expression with someone unpleasant from our past.

It can be said, then, that three things shape a person. The external world continually provides raw images for us to digest. The conscious mind archives and processes these images and tries to control them. The subconscious mind retains the gut reactions to the world's images, though these reactions are only partially responsive to the conscious mind's control. Without being able to break the chain of command by communicating directly with our subconscious, our unreasoned and automatic responses to events usually continue.

Guided imagery that employs relaxation allows us to communicate more directly with the subconscious. When we relax fully, physical changes take place in our bodies. Breathing becomes slow and regular, pulse rate decreases, and body temperature drops. The brain stops producing active beta waves and begins to emit the slower alpha waves, which means the mind can shift more easily from one level of thought or memory to another. As we relax and unwind, the conscious mind is put at ease and visiting images are allowed to enter.

Imagery allows us to create a familiar, safe, and relatively controlled environment that is unlikely to raise anxiety and force us to react mechanically. The relaxed mind can choose among familiar concepts and experiences, creating new settings in which to exercise feelings and knowledge. In the safety of guided imagery, our minds can open to the spontaneous images that surface in it, possibly making us aware of significant abilities and attributes or illuminating suppressed anxieties.

The conscious mind, however, is still there and can come to the rescue if any threat arises. The conscious mind's ability to protect us makes guided imagery a safe and natural technique.

What is imagery? You are more familiar with it than you may think. Any conscious, awake human can re-create an experience, if only for an instant, in their mind's eye. You can recall the way your bedroom looks without being in it. You can replay parts of a favorite tune when the radio is off. In the middle of the summer, you can visualize what snow looks and feels like. You can taste chocolate ice cream before you get to the store. These are common examples of visualization, which is a form of mental imagery.

More intensely, but generally not under our control, most of us experience nondirected imagery when we dream. In dreams you may "see" sights you have never seen before, encounter people who are actually hundreds of miles away, and engage in strenuous physical activity while lying almost completely immobile in bed.

Dreams are often the subconscious mind's random reactions to our life's experiences. Although the subconscious speaks to us through our dreams, it can be difficult to interpret what it is saying. Through guided imagery, we can influence the subconscious more directly and work on specific issues of our choosing. Guided imagery allows us to gain some control and discipline over our subconscious mind's emotional reactions.

By developing visualization skills, we can help our subconscious mind become more mature as well, and thereby gain a better understanding of who we are and what we value.

Resources on imagery & hypnosis

Alman, Brian. *The Complete Manual for Health and Self-Change.* New York: Bruner, Mazel, Inc., 1992.

Dienstfrey, Horns. *Where the Mind Meets the Body.* New York: HarperCollins Publishers, 1991.

Erickson, Milton H. *Creative Choice in Hypnosis.* New York: Irvington Publishers, 1992.

Fisher, Stanley. *Discovering the Power of Self-Hypnosis.* New York: HarperCollins Publishers, 1992.

Fromm, Ericka. *Contemporary Hypnosis Research.* New York: Gilford Press, 1992.

Gawain, Shakti. *Meditations: Creative Visualization & Meditative Exercises.* San Rafael: New World Library, 1991.

Heiberg, Jeanne. *Winning Your Inner Battle.* San Jose: Resource Publications, Inc., 1989.

Holmes, Fenwicke L. *Visualization & Concentration.* Santa Fe: Sun Publishing Company, 1992.

Johnson, Robert. *Inner Work.* San Francisco: Harper, 1986.

King, Viki. *Beyond Visualization.* San Rafael: New World Library, 1992.

Leuner, Hanscarl. *Guided Affective Imagery.* New York: Thieme Medical Publishers, Inc., 1984.

Moen, Larry. *Guided Imagery.* Naples: United States Publishing, 1992.

Murdock, Maureen. *Spinning Inward.* Boston: Shambhala Publications, Inc., 1987.

O'Hanlon, William H. *Solution Oriented Hypnosis.* New York: Norton, W. W., and Company, 1992.

Sources for New Age music

Big Sur Recordings, P.O. Box 91, Big Sur, CA 93920

Celestial Harmonies, 605 Ridgefield Road, Wilton, CT 06897

Halpern Sounds Rx. P.O. Box 2644, San Anselmo, CA 94960

Narada Productions, 1845 N Farwell Avenue, Milwaukee, WI 53202

Rounder Records, One Camp Street, Cambridge, MA 02140

Warner/Elektra/Atlantic Corp., 111 N Hollywood Way, Burbank, CA 91505

Windham Hill Productions Inc., P.O. Box 9388, Stanford, CA 94305

Invitation to readers

How often have you closed a book, wishing you could immediately share your reactions with the author? Very few of us have pursued this desire. Time and effort are usually needed to track down the author, and the end result is often a form letter or no reply at all.

I, however, am extremely interested in your reactions and questions and am offering you an opportunity to write to me and in most cases to receive a response. Please include a self-addressed stamped envelope with your correspondence.

I invite all professionals to submit for review a successful session in which imagery was used. I offer no financial reimbursement nor do I guarantee that your material will be published. Should your submission be chosen for publication, you will gain a means of sharing your knowledge and experience. Please contact me at the following address:

> Andrew E. Schwartz (Inquire Within)
> Post Office Box 228
> Waverley, MA 02179-9998

Whole Person Associates

Whole Person Associates publishes materials focused on stress management, wellness promotion, and personal growth. Our structured exercises for workshops and groups, relaxation audiotapes, workshops-in-a-book, and interactive video programs are designed for personal and professional use. Trainers, consultants, educators, therapists, psychologists, and wellness coordinators use our products in hospitals, corporate wellness programs, health care facilities, EAPs, colleges, drug and alcohol abuse programs, and in private practice. Call or write for our free catalog.

Whole Person Associates Inc
210 West Michigan
Duluth, MN 55802-1908
(218) 727-0500